The Way of Trance

Dennis R. Wier

Strategic Book Publishing
New York, New York

Strategic Book Publishing
An imprint of Writers Literary & Publishing Services, Inc.
845 Third Avenue, 6th Floor – 6016
New York, NY 10022
http://www.strategicbookpublishing.com

ISBN: 978-1-60860-089-2
          1-60860-089-11

Printed in the United States of America

Book Design: Suzanne Kelly

Table of Contents

Acknowledgments

I WISH TO THANK HILDA PERROTT, PH.D., for her help in editing the first version of this book and for helping me to add clarity to areas that only I understood. And finally, my loving thanks to Doris Wier, my wife, for her patience and support.

Introduction

TRANCE BEGAN TO INTEREST ME WHEN, in 1957, a friend and I went to see a hypnotist so I could learn to hypnotize him. I subsequently became fascinated by hypnosis and inner states. That, eventually, lead me to study yoga.

Around 1965, I started to meditate regularly. I was curious about the altered states of consciousness of yogis, but could not find any really satisfactory explanations for what these states were nor how they were created.

During the next thirty years, I developed a model for trance as I understood it, and published my first book *Trance: from Magic to Technology*. I wrote what I wanted to write, and I was personally satisfied with the book when it was published in 1995. While I felt that the book reflected my understanding of trance up until that point, I knew that the trance model itself only had been tested on me.

My first book raised much interest in ways I had not foreseen. Before the book left the printers, a manuscript of it was circulating in the psychology department of a liberal arts college. Something in that book helped a student understand trance sufficiently to stop an unterminated hypnotic trance. This was the first of several instances in which readers used the information in my book to understand and terminate personal or dangerous trances.

I was very pleased that readers could use the information in my book to help themselves. Yet the book also raised additional questions for readers, and I became quite busy answering them. I was inspired to continue my personal research with the model. I realized that trance research represents a huge task with many paths—more than I could personally explore—so I needed to involve more people in trance research.

Eventually, I opened a practice for Trance Analysis. With my clients, I learned how to apply the Trance Model in new and different ways. They also seemed to profit from this approach. I learned that the Trance Model seemed to have its greatest potential in providing a new and interesting perspective for clients with experience in meditation.

This book expands on the Trance Model and adds more detail in order to clarify many areas. Some of the subjects in this book were suggested by the interest shown during e-mail exchanges with readers and clients. This book aims to add to a growing wealth of information about trance, while being of practical use.

This book does not aspire to provide definitive and rigid answers about a complex subject; rather, it is a "way of trance," more like a map of my own explorations, which you might use yourself. Because this is a huge trance mountain, we all can climb and explore it. Actually, you have to do it personally yourself; I can't do it for you.

The first book was very technical and mathematical. You will find no math in this book. If you wish to study the current mathematical Trance Model, it is now a separate publication available through the Trance Research Foundation.

You might find some parts of this book abstract, and I might use a few words that could send you running to the dictionary. I really have tried to make this book personal, practical, and usable in describing a very complex and subtle subject. I have tried to keep my descriptions as precise as possible and to dilute the abstractions with as many practical examples as possible. I certainly don't have all the answers and I am still learning myself.

You may find some parts of this book provocative and even controversial. My purpose is to illuminate aspects of trance that deserve especially serious and critical attention. Presenting these aspects in provocative ways is an efficient way to expose inherent dangers.

This book's goal is to provide a clear and simple understanding of trance and its many forms. There are many subtle aspects of trance that can only be discovered directly by personal contemplation. I have tried to include pointers to these subtle aspects where appropriate. There are some important questions and exercises that may be used for group discussion. Most of the questions don't have clear answers, but they may stimulate you to imagine the possibilities of trance research and encourage you to begin to find your own way. I am convinced that along the path of personal inner exploration, many new and valuable skills can be developed.

Dennis R. Wier
Berkeley, California
April, 2009

The Way of Trance

Is This the Way to the Path?

This is a book about trance: what a trance is, how it is used, and how to get into and out of a trance safely. It is not a cookbook with recipes, although you can use what you learn here to make your own trance recipes. There are exercises and questions at the end of some chapters to make what you learn practical. Trance deals with subtleties.

I have studied and practiced trance for many decades, with many personal meditation, hypnotic, and addictive experiments. Over these many decades my definition of trance has evolved as a direct result of a regular process of deep meditation, visualization, and hypnotic experimentation, along with a rigorous application of systems analysis to interpret my experiences and refine my understanding of what has been happening. This technique of careful inner research[1] has resulted in the development of a model for trance. I also tested the Trance Model along the way with willing clients in a variety of personal situations. My clients reported that the model worked for them.

My idea of trance, as it has evolved, may be different than yours. So, in this book I make my definition and ideas as clear as I can.

I realize that different life experiences can create different ideas about the nature of the mind. My idea of trance, being a

---

[1] My own personal inner research occasionally led me into scary situations. In some ways it was like walking along the edge of a cliff in the dark without a map or knowing what I might find with my next step. I was always careful to limit such explorations through strict time limits and plenty of psychic "grounding," so that I had a safe way back.

subjective product of mind, does not represent any kind of path to enlightenment. If I have learned anything about the mind via my personal experiences with meditation, it is that "the map is not the territory." A map is useful and makes much more sense if you are actually there—in the territory and on the ground—making your own way by actual inner exploration. If you are, then this book might prove useful to you.

Some of the ideas in this book are actually very old. In terms of the development of ideas, some concepts that I describe here might remind you of ancient Hermetic principles and are expressed as my actual, direct, and first-hand personal experiences. It is not re-hashed alchemy. There is no requirement of belief and no necessity for blind faith. There is no dogma and no interpretive necessity. You are invited to create your own experiments and proof.

For most people, trance is not a subject of any compelling interest. Most people are concerned with survival. Some days the activity is work. Other days it is play. In between, they may enjoy a movie or watch some TV. On weekends, they may go to a bar, a dance, or visit friends and lovers. Life is mostly repetitive. The sun comes up; the sun goes down. The mind is generally filled with all sorts of thoughts, memories, and fantasies. Often, our main effort in life is to make those fantasies real. Most people use trance to help make those fantasies real, but they might not be aware of what they are doing. Sadly, many problems come from this basic ignorance.

If you believe that trance is a special state, you are not wrong. But it is much more common than you may recognize. A daydream is a trance, and who does not go into a daydream every day, even though you usually do not remember when or even if you did? Listening to music, a spouse, or children at play can put many people into a trance. Your spouse talks to you. Doesn't he or she, or do you not remember? And if you watch TV, commute to work, or ride in an elevator, you are probably in a trance. Because trance is so commonplace, we often don't give it much attention as a subject.

If you are in a painful situation and want to be somewhere else, and can't be, the easiest way to make the escape is to go into a trance. Trance is most often used as pain relief. The use of television is an example of trance to escape from pain. If you are in a physical or psychological prison, the easiest way to escape is with a trance.

You may remember the last time you danced. Perhaps you were young and anxious about looking good or dancing well with your partner. The rhythmic movement of a dance can produce a trance in which you are not embarrassed, not anxious about dancing, and you may even feel as though it is not you who are dancing, but you are observing yourself dancing. This is an example of a trance. Once you learn how to identify a trance, you will discover how plentiful trances are.

If you can go into a trance consciously, deliberately, with a clear goal to accomplish, and you are successful, you are on the way of trance. You can also learn with this book other methods for going into a trance and controlling the trance. One of the main purposes of this book is to promote trance awareness.

Trance is everywhere, but not usually[2] equal everywhere. People go in and out of trance many times per day—if not per hour—and in the process unconsciously create uncontrolled trances. Such uncontrolled trances can create many problems, including addictions. In order to avoid these problems, you need to know what a trance is and how it works. We can study trance with several goals in mind.

Our first goal is to be able to recognize what a trance is and what it produces as effects. Our second goal is to be able to terminate any trance and to understand why some trances are easy and others are almost impossible to terminate. And our third goal is to be able to modify a trance. Once we can recognize,

---

[2] While TV can put most people in the same room in the same trance; an electronic ultrasonic induction apparatus can put most people within several acres into the same trance.

terminate, and modify a trance, we can—when we get skill-ful—create whatever trance we like. At that point, with much more practice, trance starts to get really interesting.

The ideas of trance and the Trance Model described here are not merely abstract. These ideas are very practical and can be applied over and over in increasing levels of subtlety and com-plexity. Learning to apply the trance model is one of the ways you can participate in meditation research.

The Way

In a funny way, the way of trance goes in a circle. Every trip around the circle brings new information and experience. There is much repetition, but the hidden, obscure path followed many times, at first uncertainly and then more familiarly, begins to distinguish itself. This path, while at first seeming completely arbitrary and random like the stars in the sky, begins to show itself in multiple patterns. The shaman's drum, the priest's incantations, the yogi meditating in the woods, the Dionysian trance party, the soldier in the killing field, the programmer in his cubicle—they all can be in a trance, repeatedly going deep inside, seeking the subtle and fine reality that is just beyond our normal ken. In doing this kind of internal magic, they generate a kind of energy that can be palpable and can influence others. The energy is the "wyrd."[3] You might never be sure you are getting anywhere; it is a mystery of mysteries.

At the end of this path it might seem like you don't get anywhere in particular—it is like meditation. You meditate for years. You don't feel any different, and who is qualified to know how you change? And yet, funny things seem to happen in your life; something like magic begins to happen. Lots of telepathic experiences, the stuff of dreams become tangible in a certain way and you can see the future. You begin to experience the oneness of life.

---

[3] Special terms are defined in the Glossary and more fully explained in the text.

I think that in some sense long term meditation, like long term trance, transforms the person by allowing a deep familiarization with the inner, subtle worlds. Dealing with the thoughts, feelings, perceptions, ideas, and realities that come from someplace else—over a long period of time—and repeating this path over decades means you don't trip over the same rocks or the same sticks all of the time. Your feet grow eyes. Your arms can reach around the world. You can listen to the stars and they have messages for you. That is what trance is about.

What is a Trance?

The Map

Many years ago in a small village in the mountains of northern India, I met a man who enticed me into paying him to enter a trance, so that he could read my fortune. I agreed. After a minute or two his eyes fluttered and rolled back in his head. His body shuttered gently and some saliva began to form at his lips and dripped onto his shirt. When he first started to speak, I couldn't understand him; the words didn't make any sense. Eventually he began to speak understandable English and told me many unique and personal things, which he could not possibly have known. I was amazed and intrigued. How did he do this magic? Or was it merely a trick of deception?

Some years later, I was at a trance dance party in San Francisco. The intent was to enter a trance, let it be and follow it, and see where it goes. Some people—including myself—entered into a so-called altered state of consciousness, a trance, while dancing to the monotonous polyrhythms. After dancing for at least an hour, something happened, energies changed, and a different reality of possibilities opened. I could sense people on another level. I spent some time working with these energies. Perhaps other people were working with mine, with that of others, with themselves. I am sure many people's destinies changed. Certainly, things got moved around. Were there miraculous healings of diseases which no one knew about? Were some people changed in ways that made them decide to follow a different life path? How could simple dancing do this?

A network engineer I once met was focused on a complex array of computers, access points, backhauls, and bandwidth. His mind was so concentrated on a problem that he did not realize I was there. When he finally noticed me, he was startled. He apologized for being in a trance. Yet, while in this trance, he accessed powerful and creative problem-solving skills. The solutions he discovered while in his trance, changed the network access destinies of hundreds of people. It was certainly nothing he had to apologize for. He was like a shaman doing magic.

Another time while in New York City I passed a building where a number of alcoholics and junkies congregated on the steps. Many had long hair; most had dirty clothes; and the smell of alcohol, stale urine, and sweat was overpowering. But I stopped and spoke to one of them. He was coherent to a point, but he repeated the same phrases with an affect that was out of context. He was seemingly stuck in a compulsive trance state. His destiny surely had changed from what it had been before he became an alcoholic. His options were now so limited that his life was being squeezed out of him. It was a trance but not a good one.

A medical doctor I know in Switzerland uses muscle testing and aura reading along with more ordinary medical methods to enhance his sensitivity to his patients as well as to the medicines he prescribes. In so doing he treats the holistic patient: their body, mind, and soul. His practice flourishes, and he is known locally more as a healer than as a doctor. The trances he enters multiple times each day influence the destinies of his patients and aid his personal research.

A doctor in California injects a patient with a drug and then the patient exhibits all the characteristics we associate with trance: fixed-eyed stare, enhanced inner involvement, and short-term amnesia. But the patient retains the ability to move and follow directions during a medical procedure.

An experimental psychologist working for the US Army uses microwave and ultrasonic electronics to transmit hypnotic commands to a group of army recruits and discovers that over twenty percent of them will follow the hypnotic commands, even though none of the recruits consciously heard the hypnotic suggestions nor showed any outward signs of being in a hypnotic trance. While an army psychologist might have the best interests of recruits at heart in an experimental situation, what prevents other people from using the same technology if their motives were not benign?

With powerful trance inducers such as drugs and ultrasonically induced trance, what does the future hold for us as individuals? Will you be able to distinguish between "true love" and hypnotically created "love?"

Outside influences change our destiny by altering the way we perceive or process information. In a similar way, when our perception and cognition remains constant or is reduced, restricted, or confined to a few limited choices, our potential for action and our potential for change is also reduced, restricted, or confined. Our destiny is our potential. Any time we increase or decrease our potential for change or expand or limit our choices, we influence our destiny.

Although it seems that the above examples are different, they all have commonalities. Once you begin to understand the elements of trance, you will also understand how to recognize, create, and control trances. Trance seems to follow a different kind of physics than normal—the energies are different, unusual. In fact, the physics of trance seems more quantum than Newtonian in the sense that the concepts, causes, and effects of space and time may be altered.

There is a connection between trance and destiny. If you can become familiar with trance, you can change your destiny. Yet, it seems you must penetrate a taboo in order to have any success with trance. Certainly you must get over any fear of trance.

The Approach

Trance is more of a common rather than a rare phenomenon. There are many kinds of trance, and each trance may present itself differently and can exhibit many different strengths or powers. Because of these variations, trance presents a rather complex subject for study. The investigation of trance is subjective, internal, personal, and transforming. I will try to explain my understanding of trance as clearly as possible as well as the reasons for my perspective.

In order to precisely understand what a trance is, you need to define the simplest minimum number of commonalities of trance-related phenomena, and then classify different trance types according to these defined commonalities. This approach is nothing more than applying the scientific method by seeking the fewest number of variables to explain phenomena and then following the implications. What is radically different from the scientific method is that we ourselves are both the object and subject of our experimentation. In this sense, what we are doing has much in common with alchemy.

There is one thing you do need to know: trances can be built within or added to preexisting trances. In other words, you can start with a simple meditation trance and then add a hypnotic trance. Or you can start with one meditation trance form and then introduce another form of meditation. Or you can start with a hypnotic ritual trance and then add multiple meditation trances. It is almost like making a soup: start with one main ingredient, then later add other ingredients to change the taste or nutritive effects. You can do it, but you need to know what you are doing. You can certainly create powerful effects with complex trances, but you can also create a terrible mess if you don't know what you are doing. Of course no ethical teacher of meditation will have you start doing these complex forms of meditation at the beginning of your practice, just as you don't enter a car race as soon as you have learned to drive. Even ancient texts on yoga warn of the dangers of practicing meditation without proper preparation and instruction.

It is fairly easy to create these complex trance systems; just start one trance after another. But the problem is that each new trance has a synergistic effect on other previously created or preexisting or unterminated trances. Even simple trance systems can rapidly become complex entities and influence our behavior in many unexpected ways. There are many common words that describe such complex trance systems, such as habits, beliefs, delusions, addictions, devotion, and "crazy-

19

as-a-loon." If you want to understand a particular complex trance, then deconstruct its complexity by identifying each underlying trance, its method of creation, and its individual as well as synergistic effects. I will later explain why all of these can be understood better if you consider them to be different forms of a trance.

Trances also can be both benign or malign. Usually, but not always, the trances we deliberately and consciously create for ourselves are benign. At least we have some initial control over them and they are non-invasive. Trances you create in error or unconsciously may result in the establishment of foolish ideas, beliefs, or delusions over which you have little control. Trances created by others against our will or judgment are almost always not to our personal benefit; I term this trance abuse. Being able to identify both what creates a trance as well as its effects and being able to intervene in order to terminate an unwanted trance is the minimum we should demand of ourselves.

Once you know how trances are created and how to identify a trance and terminate it, you might like to develop some useful trance skills. Trance is very useful for accelerated learning and can create powerful healing energy for ourselves and others. Becoming a master at creating trance in ourselves and others may be a key for manifesting new ideas, art, music, dance, engineering, as well as financial and personal success. Trance can also help promote healing in ourselves and others. Indeed, the lack of effective trance skills can become a formidable barrier to success in life. If you don't know what a trance is and how it works, you can easily fall under the spell of a salesman, priest, magician, or politician who may not have your best interests at heart!

Before defining what a trance is, you need to know in more detail what you do when you think, decide things, and how you understand what reality is. You can then begin to explore how trance creates other possibilities, other realities, and other destinies—because that's what it does.

So, you can see that the "way of trance" is not necessarily a simple idea. However, you will find some familiar conceptual landmarks along the way, and these will help to clarify our understanding.

I will now discuss the ordinary way you think and experience life using some terms from psychology.

Cognitive Objects

Cognitive objects are something slightly more complex than a thought, a feeling, or an inner sense, yet cognitive objects are certainly what you ordinarily think of as words. Cognitive objects rattle around in our heads all of the time. In general, cognitive objects come and go from our awareness without much effort on our part. But they make up most—if not all—of our internal world. Cognitive objects are also what you work with when you work with trance. I use the term cognitive object rather than thought, because most people associate a thought with words; I specifically want to include feelings and non-thought-like internal sensations. Subtle, vague feelings become more important than words for trance work, and many subtle feelings have no words and often cannot be easily described. But they are all cognitive objects.

The Energy Involved in Thinking

For most people, thinking—the process of going from one cognitive object to another—seems effortless. A moment's reflection will indicate that it is not. For some, thinking logically can be an effort; for others, thinking emotionally can be an effort. For some people remembering where they put their car keys is an effort. Thinking in specific ways with which we are not familiar, often requires more mental energy than we are used to.

The path most of our thoughts take is usually the path of least resistance. You love the familiar, and so you think the same thoughts or at least thoughts you like. This is because the energy you have available for thinking is a limiting factor. The more available energy you have, the better you can think.

21

Changing the amount of energy available for thinking, therefore, changes the way you think. Trance is really a way of modifying the energy in our heads, so that you can think in different ways. You actually do this all of the time. When you feed the cat, you are using one kind of energy, but when you balance your checkbook, you have modified your thinking patterns by changing the allocation of cognitive energy. If it is easy to change this energy, you think nothing of it. If it is difficult to change the energy or you don't know how to do it, you can learn how to do it. And yet, some new thinking patterns may be impossible. Or you simply put off what you don't have the mental energy for. And some people, when blocked because of low energy resources, use self-destructive strategies to get their needs met in fantasy if not in reality.

For example, loading oneself up with alcohol or drugs clearly changes one's energy. It may focus our will, enable us to take high risks, and it might result in a successful strategy, for awhile. But it might also become a very unsuccessful strategy. Stress and worry also change energy demands. Many people believe that if one is stressed enough, as it focuses will and enables one to take high risks, one can eventually succeed. There are many other external ways to change the available energy you have for thinking. If you could willfully modify your energy in other ways, you might make those changes in your thinking.

One way that you can modify the energy for thinking is by repetition. If you do something often enough, you will learn it, and it will become easier—second nature to you. This gives us a critical key to know how a trance is created: by the repetition of cognitive objects. We will examine repetition in more detail because it is a principle way that a trance is created. There are other ways as well—drugs, trauma, illness, fear, etc. But for now, let us just consider repetition. It's much more benign.

Loops

If you reflect on your thought processes for a moment, you will find that many thoughts repeat. So do your feelings. Much of life is a sequence of repetitions, from brushing your teeth to going to work, from music listening to making love.

We can often learn a skill by going through its technique multiple times until the skill becomes easier. This repetition—also a cognitive loop—is the common factor whether you are learning to tie your shoes, learning a new language, shooting a gun, practicing your stroke, or learning a new surgical technique. Basically, you practice it over and over until you learn it, and it becomes second nature.

Learning anything is also a way of saving energy. Once you learn how to multiply two numbers together, you don't need to count on your fingers and toes any longer. Repeating a set of cognitive objects in order to learn something is how most people learn. You repeat certain physical movements in order to learn how to drive a car. At some point, you have repeated a set of movements so many times that a specific action becomes simple, automatic, and second nature to you, which means that you have saved mental processing energy. Part of you doesn't need to go through the specific details of the action, and you have gained another skill. Some people have even streamlined the learning process in such a way that they learn faster with a minimum of repetition.

What is "second" nature? Another reality? Does your destiny change when you learn a new skill? Loops are, in fact, the fundamental building blocks of trance. You can see where this is going, can't you? There is a connection between cognitive objects, cognitive loops, energy, trance, and changing your destiny. There are some other important details to consider as well.

A bit about destiny: if you always do things the same way with the same conditions, the results will most likely be the same. Your destiny does not change in that case. But if conditions change you might be compelled—through a new expenditure of energy—to change the way you do things, and, consequently, the results will also change. Your destiny changes in relation to how you can manage the energy requirements of changing conditions.

The Content of a Loop

Besides the structural fact that a loop is a topological circle and circles are round and repeat, another important part of a loop is its contents. So, all loops have both a circular structure and enumerable sequential contents.

One way to represent or describe a loop is by naming its contents and thinking of the contents as a finite ordered list or a closed ordered set. There are other ways to represent loops, but this is a simple but essential first step in describing the kind of mental loop that creates a trance.

Cognitive Functions

As commonly understood by psychologists, cognitive functions are specific thinking processes. Some of the common cognitive functions are: critical judgment, short term memory, body awareness, mathematical processing, literalism, inner visualization, awareness of reality, etc. Some so-called occult or magical functions of the mind—although rare—are also cognitive functions. These are: clairvoyance, telekinesis, remote viewing, healing powers, controlling the autonomous physical systems of the body, foreseeing the future and all the yogic siddhis, etc. In fact, there are so many examples of cognitive functions that it may be a formidable task to enumerate and precisely describe them all.

Anyway, it is not very helpful to create a definition by means of multiple examples, especially when I have not really described what a cognitive function is. We need a more precise definition of cognitive function for trance.

What is a Cognitive Function?

We have seen that cognitive objects are connected to each other in ways that define a function or reflect an on-going thought process or transformation. The on-going process may result from sensory input or may be derived, trained, or learned.

If a thought is bouncing around in one's head, the domain is the area of the originating cognitive object, the bouncing is the function, and the area of the resulting cognitive object is the range. There are two limits or areas in a cognitive function. First are the set of cognitive objects that a cognitive function uses as input, and second is the range of a cognitive function's results. Normally, there is a limit to the range of any cognitive function and there is a natural resistance to going beyond that limit.

Let us assume, for example, that there is a named cognitive function called "reacting to fire." And that this cognitive function uses skin temperature sensing as its input domain, and muscle jerking as its output range. If I placed a lighted match under your outstretched hand, the "reacting to fire" cognitive function would cause your hand to jerk away if the cognitive function were working properly. By properly I mean that the energy expended for this correctly functioning cognitive function is minimal. One can imagine that if the cognitive function were rewired in some way—that is, by adding energy to the cognitive function through training or hypnosis—a lighted match under the hand might only cause the eyelids to blink rapidly. Or processing of the input domain could be modified so that merely touching the palm would cause a muscle jerk reaction, as though you had felt fire. Changing the way a specific cognitive function operates is one of the expected goals of trance.

Now let us consider another cognitive function. If I asked you what two plus five equals, the two and the five are in the domain of cognitive objects you can add, the plus is the transformation function within the arithmetic cognitive function, and the answer cognitive object—seven—is in the range of actual answers. Our idea of a cognitive function has the concept of truth or correctness connected with it, trained in, over time, in elementary school. If you said that two plus five is ten, then the normal plus function for you in that case has failed. Although ten is still within the range of the cognitive function—ten is a number, after all—the given answer is outside the range of validity for the arithmetic "plus" cognitive function in this specific instance. Notice that we are now talking about two different cognitive functions. There is the arithmetic cognitive function of plus, which associates two cognitive objects with a third to produce something called an answer, and there is a second cognitive function, which assigns reality to the process of the first cognitive function and validates it. So, two plus five equals seven is right, and two plus five equals ten is wrong. If you add some teaching energy to the wrong process, you might be able to change the function so that it works correctly. This difference in energy is what you add to an immature non-adding child to change the destiny of that child to become empowered to add numbers correctly. We don't usually think of the fact that you are changing the destiny of the child when you teach him to add correctly, but you can agree that when a child can add correctly, it gives that child a life-long benefit.

Our purpose in discussing the arithmetic cognitive function in such detail is to describe a subtle difference between ordinary thinking and thinking while in a trance. If you were in a trance, you might think that two plus five is twenty five and this might be a perfectly acceptable answer (right!) for someone in such a dream world. But this answer is outside the reality or range of what you normally consider to be correct answers for the arithmetic cognitive function. So, when you witness this fact from our ordinary or normal reality, you say that the arithmetic cognitive function has failed and the answer is wrong. This simply means that the answer is outside of what you normally think of as correct. It is not an ethical failure, but merely a processing failure for that specific cognitive function that put it out of the reality range of the normal. Generally, by training and habit—which is to say, a long-term trance—we prefer to stay within the range of correct arithmetic cognitive functions. There is a reluctance and resistance to break the law of training and habit of correct arithmetical form and function. But being in a trance makes it easy to break this law. So, there is something about trance that changes our potential, our destiny. Trance, in fact, enabled us to learn how to add correctly and can also enable us to access other realities in which "addition" itself changes meaning.

Although I was describing the arithmetic cognitive function, the same observations can be made about any other cognitive function. That is, you assign a certain reality value to the result of a cognitive function, which is arbitrary. The collective result of these assignments gives us the gestalt of our reality and explains why you normally can't talk to plants or to our ancestors. This means if you want to see spirits, for example, you will have to conditionally rewire the way your cognitive functions operate while maintaining some kind of control. The disciplined practice of meditation over many years often results in exactly this type of control.

The Effect of a Loop on a Cognitive Function

Now I'd like to consider how cognitive functions are affected by cognitive object loops. When thinking normally, there are few or no loops. You process one thought after another. Repetition does happen, but the repetition is not normally sustained within a short time frame, nor repeated multiple times. But there is an obvious effect on cognitive functions when short loops are repeated. You can prove this to yourself easily. Imagine I asked you "What is seven plus four?" over and over again. You might first get bored, and then, perhaps, angry. At some point[4] you naturally begin to doubt the reality of your answer, or you doubt that you are adding correctly. The repetition drives you a little crazy. You would consider the repetition of the question as little more than torture.[5]

When any set of thoughts repeat, then cognitive functions stop functioning normally. You can prove this assertion in your own mind. If you think the word fish over and over, part of your mind will select—perhaps—first an image of the animal, fish; then the verb, to fish; then the memory of the smell of fish; then funny ways to spell fish; then memories of fishing on a boat;

---

[4] How many repetitions it takes before you get to this point would be a measurement of the strength of the trance which is created.
[5] Some people get bored with the repeating musical notes of trance music; it can even be torture for some people.

then fishing for compliments; then word play, puns; and finally the word fish might get to be meaningless, simply a sound, as your mind fills with rich associations and goes outside of the range of normal associations.

What happens is that repeating a set of cognitive objects has caused you to dissociate. You suspend your critical judgment and begin to doubt your current model of reality. You begin to become open, suggestible to other realities. Maybe, seven plus four is twenty-nine. Could it be? Why not break the taboo of staying in this reality and "add" in another way?

Resistance of the Range

There is, of course, a resistance to altering a cognitive function. How many times do you need to be told that "seven plus four is forty-seven?" before you finally get it? Ten times? Fifty times? Ten thousand times? Believe me, there is a number—I don't know what it is—but at some point you will believe that "seven plus four is forty-seven." The number of repetitions that it takes before you accept a new reality is related to the resistance of the cognitive function to modification. Every cognitive function has such a resistance. This resistance is not usually tested, but sometimes it is. Cognitive loops tend to bang on the wall of resistance, and in time the wall breaks. At that point the cognitive function becomes amenable to change and after that functions differently.

If the arithmetic cognitive function has a sort of durability (high resistance) in your head, that is normal. But cognitive functions such as short term memory can fail in accuracy (low resistance) more often than you would think. Yet people will accept the result of a faulty memory with not much more than a shrug or an "oh well." One does this because short term memory in most instances need not be infallible. In other words, people can tolerate short term memory error and failure, except, perhaps, on exams or when searching for the car keys. But a loose grip on short term memory is valuable if you want to fantasize or think outside of the box.

We can test the resistance of the part of a cognitive function that assigns reality to the cognitive function. There are simple psychological tests, for example, for determining the accuracy of your short term memory or how well you can do math. The hand levitation test, used by hypnotists, is a simple means of determining hypnosis, but it really is a measure of the resistance of a specific cognitive function. Any hypnotic trance can alter some specific cognitive functions, thus standardized tests can be designed to measure the resistance of these cognitive functions.

Cohesiveness of Associations

The "cohesiveness of association" is not a common subject for psychologists, but the "cohesiveness of association" reflects a capacity for meaning. You may associate cat with mouse more easily than cat with mortgage, because the cognitive objects cat and mouse are more closely associated in normal day to day reality than are cat and mortgage.

To put it another way, if I say cat, you are more likely to say mouse than mortgage, and I could with some experimentation come up with number values or probabilities that reflect the difference in associative closeness between cat and mouse as opposed to cat and mortgage. You could say that cat and mouse are more meaningfully connected than are cat and mortgage, that is, more cohesive conceptually.

The "cohesiveness of association" also extends to non-verbal cognitive objects although measuring the cohesiveness of meaning is more problematic. For example, what do you associate with the sight of blood? The sight of blood is strongly associated with fear and only arguably slightly less associated with mortgages. So the "cohesiveness of association" for non-verbal cognitive objects is still connected with the capacity for meaning, although it may be more difficult to measure.

You may notice in your own mind at this point, that because of the repetition of sentences with the words cat and mortgage in them, that you may begin to associate cat with mortgage and begin to wonder if, perhaps in another reality, they might be related.

When the "cohesiveness of association" of cognitive objects is somewhat high, then you think in a normal, prudent, mature, perhaps even a conservative way; a lower "cohesiveness of association" means thinking is more playful, dreamy, metaphorical, or even more poetic as association patterns become more chaotic. Extremely low "cohesiveness of association" could make us seem creative to the point of incoherence, while a very high "cohesiveness of association" makes us more literal and unable to think "outside the box."

Some cognitive functions, such as performing an addition, require a high "cohesiveness of association" of cognitive objects. Otherwise, the addition of two plus three might equal sandbox instead of five. Other cognitive functions, such as accessing a memory, require a lower "cohesiveness of association" of the cognitive objects. Whenever any cognitive function resists being modified, we identify the high "cohesiveness of association" with "normal" reality or the idea of right or correct, and a low "cohesiveness of association" with either wrong, creative thinking, or accessing other realities. Modifying the resistance of a cognitive function so that we can access other realities is one of the purposes of trance.

The Structure of Trance

Trance is a cognitive process, rather than a state of awareness. It affects awareness by modifying the resistance of cognitive functions. Trance does this as a means of changing the energy consumed or used by sets of cognitive functions. Subjectively, in a trance, you experience reality in a variety of new ways. Practically, trance enables us to function in ways that enhance survival by opening up an awareness of other realities; so, trance is also a survival mechanism. If our day-to-day experience does not demand a change in the resistance of our cognitive functions, then we call that normal and what we experience is also normal. For this reason, most people conclude that trance is an unusual state and not normal.

The Essential Structure

Modifying the resistance of your cognitive functions happens when you are shocked, or fearful, or whenever you repeat cognitive objects. Also, you might repeat cognitive objects because you are afraid or in shock. As I have mentioned many times before and will continue to repeat,[6] the repetition of cognitive objects will induce a dissociated condition in which the "cohesiveness of association" of cognitive objects will change as well as the resistance of various cognitive functions. Subjectively, our reality changes from something "normal" to something unusual, and you can believe you are in a different state of consciousness, although you are only processing cognitive objects in a different way. You are using psychological and biological energies that you normally can not access. Because you are not familiar with this new condition, you don't usually know how to deal with it. You are afraid of it and break the trance, or with a little complexity you can get stuck in it. But if you can train yourself to handle other realities and be in a trance consciously, you can begin to use these new, usually hidden, psychological and biological energies—the wyrd. That is, you could really become after some practice somewhat magical.

Complex Structure

When a single trance is maintained over a period of time, it may change slightly and become another trance or, more likely, multiple trances. After awhile, these trances begin to accrete into more complex trance forms. How they attach or relate to each other gives different flavors to trance.

---

[6] Making a comment about text you are reading is a way of encouraging dissociation and inducing a trance. I do this as an example in order to help you become aware of how easily a trance is created. There are many other examples of inducing a trance in this book—not annotated like this one—left to your discovery, so that you may practice your skills.

For example, if you meditate until you hear the dinner bell, you have a meditation trance followed by a hypnotic trance. If your partner jabbers at you until you space out just to get away, you have a hypnotic trance followed by a meditative trance. If you train yourself to always space out when your partner jabbers at you, you will begin to have an addictive trance. It is the repetition of training that constitutes a trance generating loop, and it is this loop that makes an addiction out of combinations of a hypnotic and meditative trance.

The effects of one or more trances come from the cognitive functions that are changed and the order in which they are changed. Usually, the cognitive function of critical judgment is the first cognitive function to fail or to become disabled. After that, short term memory fails. After that comes a decrease in body awareness.

Disabled Cognitive Functions

There are many cognitive functions and some of them are always disabled during a trance. With training, the order of disabling of cognitive functions can be pre-programmed. Sleep or unconsciousness may or may not be desired during a trance, so a continuous body awareness needs to be maintained or enabled. Generally, the cognitive functions remaining enabled can be controlled by a hypnotist or through self-suggestion, or in the case of meditation, by certain postures.

With simple, short-lasting trances there is not usually a detectable change in the wyrd, because the "cohesiveness of association" does not change.

Effects on Cognitive Functions

A number of cognitive functions are disabled during any meditation. Moreover, the order in which cognitive functions are disabled will define important characteristics of the specific meditation trance. A meditation trance can result in a variety of dissociative conditions including short-term memory failure, more general temporary memory loss, disabled normal association structures, decrease in associative cohesiveness, increased literalism, disabled critical judgment, and enhanced inner involvement. It may also produce so-called delusions and/or visions of other realities. These variations can be enumerated and described more fully by reference to specific cognitive functions and the order in which they are disabled or modified.

Because this mechanism of trance creation is not generally well-known, many people make an error by wrongly associating an effect of a trance—such as staring—with the cause of trance. The cause of a trance is the repetition of cognitive objects; the effect of a trance is the set of disabled or modified cognitive functions.[7]

Short Term Memory

Short term memory is the ability to recall events which occurred in the recent past.

Although a meditation trance is always created from a trance generating loop, such as a mantra, sometimes the effect of the trance disables short-term memory or self-awareness of the trance generating loop itself. In this case, you are not aware that you are in a trance and not aware of what you did to get in the trance. In other words, you forget to repeat your mantra.

When short term memory fails, you simply don't remember the mantra. It's not there any more. You don't have an association from your current thinking, such as it is, to the recent past event that was sitting with the intent to meditate. More severe short term memory loss means that you make no association between the recent past event and your current thinking, so that even if prompted, you don't get the connection. One meditation technique to overcome this short term memory failure is to

---

[7] A strong drug, electronic or microwave stimulation, or mechanical trauma, such as a bullet in the brain, while not a repetition of a cognitive object, can also disable many cognitive functions, resulting in a massive invasive trance.

introduce the secondary trance generating loop: once you realize you forgot to repeat your mantra, start repeating it again.

Another form of short term memory failure is a false association with other cognitive objects but not the recent past event. During meditation, there is a tendency to day-dream. Somehow you know you should be meditating using a mantra, but remembering and reliving a past sexual encounter over and over is so much more fun.

In these cases the "cohesiveness of association" decreased from some normal value to a value equal to or very close to zero.

Critical Judgment

Critical judgment is the ability to see the relationship between cause and effect. Critical judgment fails when causes are correctly perceived but incorrect conclusions are made, or when causes are based on delusion, or when the connection between a cause and its effect is not made.

For example, if you know that you need air to live and you know that you cannot breathe when submersed in water, what could you conclude seeing a child face down in a swimming pool? If your critical judgment is active, you will arrive at the right conclusion right away and work to get the child out of the water and into the air. If critical judgment fails, you might think the child is playing a game or that there is a trick to breathing under water. Or although you know you need air to breathe and you cannot breathe submerged in water and a child is face down in a swimming pool, you fail to conclude or understand either that the child may be in mortal danger or that the child may have drowned.

Literalism

Literalism is resistance to metaphor. It is a way of avoiding ambiguity and complexities beyond a simple and superficial understanding. It is related to critical judgment in that literalism puts a stop to any meaningful considerations of alternative perspectives that might result from a robust exploration of causes and effects. There is, perhaps, no single word expressing the cognitive function that operates to prevent literalism, but you know that when that cognitive function fails, literalism is the effect.

Eye Movement

The eye tends to be in motion when animated by awareness. How the eye moves, its reasons for attraction or avoidance, has fascinated researchers.

We know that eye movement stops under certain conditions and that this cessation of movement indicates that outer awareness has to a certain extent been suspended.

So we generally conclude that a fixed-eye stare either indicates a trance, unconsciousness, or death.

Fixed-Eye Stare

A fixed-eye stare is characteristic of a disabled cognitive function associated with a specific kind of trance. If you stare at an object—typically a burning candle flame—the trance generating loop is the act of looking, looking, looking at the candle flame. This repeated act of looking is the cause of the resulting trance, and a characteristic of the resulting trance might be a fixed-eye stare. If a person has been in a trance before, a hypnotist might use a fixed-eye stare as a trigger to the prior trance. But the essential point I am making here is to distinguish very precisely between the cause of trance and the effect. If you want to understand how to create complex trance, you must be able to distinguish between a cause of trance, an effect of trance, and a trigger to a prior trance.

For example, the fixed-eye stare that is characteristic of a disabled cognitive function may be wrongly thought to be the cause of a trance; therefore, a hypnotist might encourage a client to fix the eyes on a point in order to cause a trance to occur.

If a trance does occur, it is because the triggering effect of the fixed-eye stare restarts a trance generating loop. It is the trance generating loop that creates the trance, not the fixed-eye stare per se. It is less certain that fixed-eye stare will create a trance; it is certain that a trance generating loop will create a trance.

The Wyrd

The wyrd is the energy needed to alter a cognitive function. When a cognitive function is operating normally, the wyrd will be zero. If a cognitive function is not operating normally, because an error in processing was made, the wyrd will become positive for that period of time that there was an error in processing.

For example, if your keys are on the table and you remember—falsely—that your keys are in your pocket, that will create a positive wyrd measure for the cognitive function responsible for short term memory. As soon as you remember where your keys are, the wyrd drops to zero again, indicating that no energy is needed to alter short term memory.

The wyrd is also that energy you feel when you are close to a powerful shaman or yogi. The hair practically stands up on your head as though you were in the presence of a powerful electric field. That is precisely the effect of the wyrd. It is also to be noted here that not everyone is affected the same way by the wyrd. To go back to the car keys for a moment: your car keys on the table may be invisible to you, but obvious to someone else. You may actually see electric energy coming out of the head of the saint, but not everyone will see the same energy. A healer or homeopath may see or sense an energy emanating from a chemical or plant extract, but not everyone can see or sense this same energy. Yet the healer or homeopath can use this information for diagnostic or treatment purposes. While the wyrd may be constant for a specific situation (a plant emanation or a yogic aura), the cognitive functions of different people in the presence of this constant wyrd will each have a different resistance to it.

If the car keys are invisible to you but visible to someone else, does this mean that you are crazy or merely that your cognitive functions are operating differently? If the aura of the saint is invisible to you but visible to someone else, does this mean the other is closer to enlightenment? What you can see or not see depends on how easily you can enable or disable various cognitive functions as well as the intensity of the wyrd. It is far easier to change your cognitive functions after some years of trance or meditation work.

Some cognitive functions must be disabled in order to enable others. In this case, the disabled cognitive function contributes to a positive wyrd, and the enabled cognitive function also contributes to a positive wyrd. The combined wyrd is more positive than a single instance of a disabled cognitive function.

When a cognitive function is disabled for a long period of time, the wyrd will become positive and stay positive until the cognitive function becomes enabled again.

Trances—whether meditation, hypnotic, addictive, charismatic, electronic-induced, or drug-induced—all create a positive wyrd. Generally, meditation produces the smallest increase, while charismatic trance produces the largest natural wyrd. Unnaturally high wyrds can be created by electronic or drug-induced trances. Physical trauma can also create very high wyrds.

Some wyrds may decrease or attenuate over time as an altered cognitive function achieves a homeostatic condition. The wyrd may even decrease back to zero. Some wyrds may increase in value over time if a particular combination of altered cognitive functions produces a chaotic hysteresis or stochastic condition.[8] For example, living with an alcoholic parent who creates chaos and emotional noise creates a trance condition in family members whose wyrd grows over time. This changes the destiny of every family member.

---

[8] Instability, unreliability, unexpected changes in cognitive functioning can occur due to drugs, alcohol, or physical causes as well as meditative and hypnotic trance gone awry.

The Measurement of the Wyrd

In a trance, the wyrd is the energy needed to break the trance or create it. This energy could be measured physically such as by the number of grams needed to force down the raised arm in a hypnotic trance, breaking the trance.

The energy can also be measured as the change in the galvanic skin response[9] when a loud noise or other shock terminates a meditation trance.

Several problems in the measurement of the wyrd occur when attempting to measure the effects of a long term addictive or charismatic trance. For example, an alcoholic may be in an addictive trance for decades. The energy needed to stop the alcoholism and to reestablish normalcy might be measured in the dollar amount needed by a clinic to create a permanent cure.

An example of the energy of a charismatic trance might be a Sufi master whose religious trance changes the lives of thousands of people. How can the wyrd in this example be measured? The total theoretical wyrd is the sum of the wyrds of each altered cognitive function for each person whose life has changed.

Addictive or charismatic trances generate large wyrds. Occult phenomena generally can occur only in this context. For example, a clairvoyant in a trance may have a wyrd measured by how often he or she is correct. If a clairvoyant continuously makes wrong predictions, the wyrd would be positive indicating an incorrect processing of a cognitive function, but if the clairvoyant is correct in a statistically significant way, it would imply positive wyrds on other cognitive functions. In the same way, the trance in remote viewing or psyops also has an associated wyrd, which may be correlated with the success of the remote viewing.

The measurement of the trance wyrd ultimately is associated with two measurable cognitive factors. The first factor depends on the time needed to traverse the loop. This factor is also dependent on the content of the loop itself. The amount of richness of association of the content adds both to the wyrd of the trance and to the time needed for loop traversal. For example, if

---

[9] An electrical voltage measured on the surface of the skin.

a word association test is given using the individual words comprising a trance generating loop, the number of seconds needed for a response is indicative of the richness of association. If I test for "mother" or "love" or "deserve," I may get more relatively higher response times than if I tested for "seven" or "anything." If I measure the response time for each element of the loop, the sum of the response times will give an indication of the time needed to traverse the loop, while taking into consideration the richness of association. Generally, the actual average measured time to traverse a loop with repetition will be more than the initial time needed to traverse the loop. When the time needed to traverse a loop is greater than the added richness of association times, then a trance can be presumed.

The second factor is how many times the loop is executed or for how many seconds the loop is sustained. If a loop is sustained for a fairly short period of time, the generated wyrd will be correspondingly less. In my work with the trance wyrd, I have found that the log of the second factor is more clearly associated with the strength of the wyrd.[10]

Taboo

Trance can be strengthened and the wyrd increased when some part of the trance is secret—or, more generally, covered—meaning that you don't talk about it. In other words, it is taboo. The trance may depend on mystery or fear, which may engender respect. These are all characteristics of a taboo. Taboo also works the other way. When there is a secret or deception, you can also look for a trance, because there will be disabled cognitive functions and repeated lies. While a secret or a cover is not a physical thing in itself, when a taboo does become physical, you can call it a talisman. A talisman embodies a secret that you may respect and venerate for its power and magic. The taboo protects the talisman

---

[10] I have used (log x)/y as a measure of the wyrd, where x is the second factor as described above and y is the first factor. This formula gives an estimated value for the trance wyrd that can be used for comparison purposes. This is all of the math you will find in this book.

from being uncovered and exposing its secret, because exposing the secret would probably break the trance. Because of this strengthening aspect of taboo, a taboo strengthens the wyrd.

What I have done here is to briefly describe trance in general. In the following chapters I will apply this model to specific kinds of trance and trance induction techniques.

There are practical considerations for each different type of trance. Some practical aspects of trance are not very nice. They victimize those who are unaware of trance techniques. I do not approve of many of the potential uses of trance; however, in exposing—that is, bringing light into the darkness, naming, and describing—these nefarious uses, I am deliberately breaking the taboo that they remain secret, so as to allow potential victims the possibility of protecting themselves. Mehr licht![11]

Exercises

1. Make a list of words like mother, love, deserve, cat, happiness, God, etc. Record all of your associations with those words. Tabulate both the associations, as well as the time that it takes to make then, that is between the stimulus and the response. Do the response times have a relation to the meaning? Are some response times shorter than others?

2. Studying a specific group or population, can you discover which words are most meaningful by evaluating the associations?

3. What happens to the response time when you repeat a word?

Questions

1. Discuss ways the results of Exercise 2 might be used in advertising, in religion, in politics, and in population control.

---

[11] "More light!" The last words spoken by Goethe, the author of Faust.

Meditation

Step Inside Your Mind

Meditation is a beautiful form of trance that has many important benefits. In the previous chapter I defined trance in general terms. Now, I will define a specific kind of trance, termed a meditation trance.

The term "meditation trance," like a hypnotic, addictive, or charismatic trance, refers to a specific cognitive loop structure, a specific use of the loop and the specific set of cognitive functions modified. This particular typology is an important tool for describing and discriminating between various other forms of trance. Basically the definition will help us discriminate between the causes and the effects of trance.

Definition of Meditation Trance

According to the Trance Model, a meditation trance is created whenever a repeating sequence (loop) of cognitive objects[12] is sustained for a period of time. Whenever such a loop is started mentally and maintained for a period of time, a specific type of dissociated condition always occurs, which results in the disabling of various cognitive functions. The order in which cognitive functions are disabled affects the resulting characteristics of the trance, as well as its effects.

You can prove this to yourself. Do you remember the last time you signed your name multiple times—say on traveler's

---

[12] Any repeating sequence of cognitive objects is also termed a Trance Generating Loop and sometimes abbreviated as TGL.

checks? After several signatures, you begin to space out, as though you can't remember what connection the signature has to you. This is dissociation. If you repeat a word several times, you begin to get bored. That is, one part of you is doing the repeating, the other part—the dissociated part—notes that the activity is boring. The dissociated part is sometimes called the Witness.

Although this is a simple definition, it has very profound implications for those who practice meditation, as well as those who study the effects of meditation.

Depending on the content of the cognitive objects in the trance generating loop and the character of the dissociative condition, several types of meditation trance can be further defined. Some examples of meditation will be described later in this chapter, which will illustrate how the content of the trance generating loop can be associated with different effects. It is not within the present scope of this book to exhaustively define all types of meditation as many religions define their own subtypes.

There are some simple observations and technical measurements that can be made on the trance generating loop causing a trance. One measurement is the actual content of the loop, how many cognitive objects are in the loop, and what is the content or nature of each of the cognitive objects. Om Mane Padme Hum might be counted as four cognitive objects each of which is a Sanskrit word; or it might be counted as six distinct syllables each of which is a cognitive object; or it may be counted as a single cognitive object.

The associations pertaining to each cognitive object and the association times further describe the trance generating loop content. For example, what does "Om" mean? What do you associate with "Om?" The answers to these questions and the time it takes you to answer reflects the cohesiveness of association relating to "Om."

Another measurement relates to how the loop is used when it is repeated: how many times is the loop repeated and how long does it take to repeat the loop once? Is the mantra repeated 108 times or 108,000 times? Does it take five seconds to repeat the loop once or does it take sixty seconds? An additional measurement is how long is the loop repeated and how often. Is the particular meditation repeated for a twenty minute period sitting twice per day for a week, or is it repeated six hours per day for ten years? The total length of time a meditation trance is practiced affects the trance wyrd. Another measurement is the speed at which a cognitive loop is repeated. Do you zip through the loop as fast as possible, or do you linger on each word?

Complex forms of meditation trance actively associate specific cognitive objects with mantras, visualizations, movements, etc.[13] The content of the loop can also be associated with chakras or feelings or physical movements, such as the breath or moving a bead on a mala[14] or rosary; they can also be associated with physical observations, such as colors, designs, letters, images, and so on. At this point in our discussion of meditation, we are not concerned with specific complexities, but with merely defining the structure and with technically describing the causes of a meditation trance. Meditation techniques actively associating a specific cognitive object (in the loop) with other (not in the loop) cognitive objects create complex forms of trance.

Other technical measurements may be made of the effects of a meditation trance. Some measurements are subjective, but may still be measurable with appropriate instrumentation.

One such measurement is the time interval, in seconds, between the start of the first repeated loop and the start of the dissociative condition. This is called the trance delta. If you sit for meditation and begin to repeat a mantra, how many seconds does it take before you become bored or feel that you are watching yourself repeat the mantra or even forgetting to repeat the mantra?

A related measurement is the time interval, in seconds, between the cessation of the trance generating loop and the normalization of all cognitive functions. This is called the trance

---

[13] Tibetan tantric meditations are examples of such complex meditation forms.
[14] A string of beads often used to count repetitions of a mantra.

epsilon. Unterminated trance results in trancelings[15] and a very high trance epsilon.

Another type of measurement relates to the character of the dissociative condition itself. Dissociation can be defined as the selected disabling of cognitive functions. One of the first cognitive functions to become disabled in a trance is critical judgment. A second cognitive function usually disabled is short term memory.[16] Body awareness is another cognitive function also among the first few common cognitive functions disabled when a trance starts. These and other cognitive functions, when noted in the order in which they become disabled, help to define more precisely the specific nature of a trance.

There are many physiological measurements of the effects of meditation that can be and have been made. It is well-known, for example, that meditation affects blood pressure, produces profound relaxation,[17] alters galvanic skin response, and has many other measurable physiological effects.

Although the detailed technical measurements of a trance may only be interesting for researchers, practical meditators should also be aware of these factors so that they don't confuse cause with effect and realize that disabled cognitive functions are normal for any trance.

Separating Causes from Effects

Some people will identify the word meditation with the effects of the meditation trance, and others will identify the word or mantra used with the causes of these effects as perceived from a trance. Thus, a meditation trance has been defined by some as a "state of ecstasy," and by others, as "grace from God." Wrongly then, through these kinds of definitions, the effects of trance are assumed to be the causes of trance. By logical extension, a belief in "God" or in "The Light" seems to be required in order

---

[15] A tranceling is any unterminated trance, usually in relation to the unexpected or undesirable effects of such unterminated trances.

[16] Some critics of meditation often cite memory failure as a reason for not meditating.

[17] Called the relaxation response by Wallace and Benson.

to have grace, ecstasy, and other effects of trance. It is the lack of a clear model of trance that has caused this confusion of cause and effect.

The Trance Model attempts to separate the causes of trance from its effects. When there is confusion of cause and effect, then there is the possibility of introducing a belief in extraneous causes or of being unclear as to the limitations of the effects.

An example of this confusion is that it is often falsely believed that some kind of divine intervention is needed in order to create specific effects of meditation or trance. The idea of divine intervention comes from projections stemming from the dissociated state that is part of the meditation trance. That is, it is not necessary to introduce the idea of divine intervention when the idea of dissociation is sufficient.

The Origin of the Other

The concept of dissociation comes from the idea that the "I" or ego is split into two parts. Which "I" then is the real "I?" Some traditions split the "I" into the "Self," or "Witness," and "the Other," or "Shadow." The Self, of course, is defined as the "real" part and the Other is believed not really to be "real" in the same sense that the Self is real. Or so it would seem, and this belief results in not a small amount of philosophical confusion.

This confusion is based on not knowing where the "I" is once the meditation trance is started. Is the "I" the cognitive loop that consciousness followed before the meditation trance came into existence? Or is the "I" the resulting dissociated trance state, which is subjectively perceived as different from the cognitive loop?

Indeed, most people will be simultaneously aware of both the "I" of the cognitive loop (the mantra, for example) and the "I" that is in a trance, but will identify the "true I" as that which exists in a trance. This "true I" has been termed the "Witness" by some religious groups. Yet, awareness in a trance always involves some disabled cognitive functions. Is then the consciousness of the "true I" also disabled?

When there is confusion as to the nature of this "Witness," then it might be easy to falsely assume that there is another entity (not the individual "I") creating the effect. The attributions given to this other mysterious entity have created a great deal of confusion and misunderstanding about the nature of the mind and the way meditation works. To clarify further, when you meditate, repetition itself will cause dissociation to occur, and this will really result in two simultaneous conscious processes. There is no single "true I" at this point; both conscious processes embody some disabled cognitive functions, which give rise to various subjective effects. There is no mysterious entity involved.

There is no reason to create any religious mumbo-jumbo about meditation unless a hidden reason for doing so is to somehow exploit the trance and to make it more than it is. Such exploitation is usually based on an abuse of the disabled critical judgment effects of the trance.

As I will discuss later, there is a cognitive function that maps a perception into an assurance that this is real or this is the truth. When this cognitive function works, then we think we know what is real. When this cognitive function fails, then what is not real can be identified as real, or what is real can be identified as not real. In other words, we can be tricked. But it is more subtle than that. Psychologically, if this cognitive function would be permanently disabled, it would constitute a pathology. In some philosophical sense, what is real really is arbitrary; it depends solely on the functioning of this specific cognitive function.

Daydreams

Meditation, as I have defined it, is certainly not limited to religious exercises. Daydreaming is also a form of meditation. This form of meditation also begins with a trance generating loop. The loop for daydreams often contains remembered elements of sight, hearing, or touch with strong emotional effect or feelings. When this feeling loop has repeated three or more times, a trance is created. Often one characteristic of the daydreaming trance is the disabling of short-term memory. The subjective effect of disabling short-term memory is that one does not remember the elements of the trance generating loop. Next time that you are in a daydream, try to remember what you did to create that dream. It is a good exercise in re-enabling your short term memory.

Another example of a meditation trance occurs whenever a phrase is repeated mentally to oneself such as "I hate my job, I hate my job, I hate my job!" This trance generating loop always creates a dissociated condition. The desired effect of the trance may be to reduce body awareness or to relieve pain associated with work. In addition, heightened visual imagination can enable power fantasies and also allows creative constructive visualization, which can have positive or beneficial effects for the job. Another effect of the trance can be to disable short term memory in which case there is no awareness of the trance generating loop. In this latter condition one's sense of reality has switched to the trance plane and can no longer be considered normal. It is, in fact, considered to be an altered state of consciousness.[18]

What is Meditation Used for?

Meditation usually creates profound feelings of deep relaxation and feelings of well-being among those who first begin to meditate, if they are taught correctly. Physiologically, meditation trance has been shown to reduce blood pressure, lower galvanic skin response, increase peripheral blood flow, and increase or enable alpha rhythms in the brain.

Because of these effects, meditation is often used to relieve stress. Business people, those in competitive sports, or in stressed relationships all can benefit from the regular practice of meditation.

These effects of meditation can be explained as resulting from specific disabled cognitive functions. When the short-term memory of anger, pain, stress, or conflict is disabled, for exam-

---

[18] A term originated by Charles Tart.

ple, there is a mediation of muscle tension in the cardiovascular system that can be subjectively experienced as a profound sense of well-being or deep relaxation. Blood pressure is also affected, and consequently, health is often affected in a beneficial way.

Who meditates and why?

Many people meditate for religious reasons. Indeed, meditation has long been associated with religious practices. Therefore monks, yogis, magicians, and witches all use meditation in order to further their aims. But meditation need not be associated with religion: Fundamentally meditation is a way to alter destiny.

Initiation into Meditation Traditions

In many traditions, a meditation student is first induced into a hypnotic trance by a meditation teacher. This hypnotic induction takes place during instruction or initiation or religious training or through performance of ritual magic. It need not be so, but generally it is this way. The purpose of the hypnotic trance is to give a student the experience of trance, and, in so doing, explicitly instruct the student on methods that are effective in recreating that same or a similar trance. It may be that because of traditions of secrecy—that is, taboo—and because of a lack of knowledge of the technology of trance, various extraneous symbols and practices have been attached to religious meditation practices. It could be for this reason that meditation techniques are often identified with some specific religious practice. In addition, the mantras or zikhr[19] or holy prayers used as part of the trance generating loop are triggers to prior ideas or concepts or to emotionally heavy events.

Initiations tend to be secret affairs, surrounded by mystery and so on. As previously mentioned, this characteristic of initiation is the taboo part of the trance. It serves to increase the wyrd or strength of the meditation trance by covering or obfuscating the hypnotic trance. It is a benign secret in most cases, but it can

---

[19]The Sufi term for a mantra or name of God or Allah.

also be a future trigger for trance abuse. Some cults with hidden agendas can easily manipulate those members who give up personal responsibility for a chance to better their own lives.

Words or triggers to emotionally heavy memories will tend to engage a person in internal mental thoughts, visions, and memories.[20] These types of word triggers make it relatively easy to establish trance in those persons who are easily drawn into such internal processes. When such triggers are chosen as mantras, it becomes especially easy to establish addictive trances. With much repetition, isolated practice, devotion, and rituals or practices anchoring somatic secondary trance generating loops,[21] these religious addictive trances can become fixed, narrow, and centric—where the most important thing in the world is the religion—with a rich range of compulsive and delusional ideas.

Generally, the use of hypnotic trance in order to instruct someone in meditation techniques has a great potential for abuse. In fact, it may be usual to introduce false causes during the instruction of meditation. Symbols, pictures and mandalas, smoke and mirrors, singing, chanting and praying, robes, and ritual with especially dramatic effect contribute to an atmosphere or setting in which it becomes easy to associate a specific religious setting with a specific technique of meditation as well as the entire range of effects of that specific meditation. The actual content of an initiation is often surrounded by secrecy and is part of the taboo of the trance. This hocus-pocus works to increase the wyrd, which also can result in "magical" or "miraculous" happenings.

Monks, Yogis, and Magicians

Meditation used by a monk is often simply the repetition of one of the names of God. Whether God exists or not is essentially

---

[20] Jesus died for your sins! is one such phrase containing triggers to guilt. Family love stories are as well. Such loops are common in the meditation loops of addictive trances. See also the chapter on Addictive Trance.

[21] By somatic, I mean rituals with much touching or pain components or whatever anchors a trance to the body.

irrelevant. From my perspective, the effect of meditation does not depend on any specific sound or pronunciation or religion.[22] However, the sounds themselves have subtle and profound meanings within a trance, that is, when perceived while in a trance. These subtle effects cannot be perceived while in a normal consciousness, so they seem "occult" or "mysterious." To better illustrate: You might be aware that if you hear a door closing while awake, you experience a certain effect. However, if you are dreaming and you hear a door closing, you might experience a "shift" of some sort, but you would not hear the actual sound of the closing of a door.

A yogi is traditionally a "scientific" explorer of inner reality. A yogi who practices meditation does so because the specific effects of his practice are known to his tradition. When the name of a god, or an aspect of a god, is used as the mantra in a specific meditation technique, it is used for the subtle effects perceived from the perspective of the trance. The surface or "normal" sound of the mantra is not the point.

A magician may practice meditation in order to clear the mental space of worldly thoughts and to focus concentration on the invoking, banishing, or influencing of subtle energies, intelligences or spirits. The subtle influences of the stars may also be important. A magician uses the same general techniques as a yogi, except that there are more talismans, that is, magically charged objects, potent with the wyrd of prior meditations and taboo to all.

A witch or shaman may practice meditation in much the same way that a magician practices meditation. The desired effect may be to obtain control over natural energies or spirits or to obtain knowledge of events or occurrences happening at a distance or over time. A witch may use plants or elements such as metals as objects of meditation in order to experience the subtle effects and energies of these materials. The chemi-

---

[22] Meditation effects can arise from many different combinations not all of which are known. For example, it is difficult to prove that a specific effect of a meditation practice is uniquely bound to a particular sound or technique and that it is not possible to produce the same specific effect by any other means.

cal or pharmaceutical properties of a plant are also subtle and may have special meaning for a chemist who investigates that knowledge space. The investigations of a monk, yogi, magician, or witch access a different knowledge space for the plant; it is the difference between what we call the "normal" world and the dream-world, which is created by a trance.

Practicing Meditation

Whether one has a pure or impure intent, the act of creative consciousness begins with concentration, discrimination, and limitation, the separation of consciousness out of chaos and the collection of the minimum number of effective means to accomplish an act. Practically, it does not matter if any element in the trance generating loop is considered "effective," pure, or impure. In the beginning, there are no magic words that are more effective than others. It is only the pure and innocent act of choice or discrimination that is necessary.

So, assume that you chose to use the mantra "Boom Tek" for arbitrary reasons; yet, the act of choosing this specific mantra is itself an act of discrimination and limitation and further concentrates your attention only on these two sounds for your trance generating loop: "Boom" and "Tek" to the exclusion of all other thought objects.

If "Boom" is not correct in some ultimate subtle sense, then the process of meditation will expose the inappropriate or incorrect nature of this thought object element. Discrimination, choice, and critical judgment are possible only before the trance is created. Once the trance is created, discrimination and critical judgment are suspended; it is no longer possible to know what is correct and what is not correct. One gets the provisions into the boat before leaving the shore. Once you have left the shore, you must live in peace with the provisions you started out with.

Once a choice has been made and the repetition has started, an intimate and mutually supportive relationship begins with the mantra and its subtle effects.

First, a choice must be made which limits, focuses, concentrates, or discriminates between a specific meditation practice and all other practices. For esoteric reasons, as given above, this is the first critical choice.

Second, the content of the loop must be chosen. The content can be a mantra, a vision or any other form such as a feeling, a movement of consciousness, a physical movement, but it must be specific and definite. It should not be a long mantra or long sequence. Long sequences tend to break the limits set by the first critical choice.

Third, the practice is started by letting awareness run through the loop. As awareness traverses multiple times, various subjective experiences will be sensed. These subjective experiences result from the trance.

Fourth, your attention and awareness should be kept, for as long as possible and as continuously as possible, on the content of the loop. To keep your attention on the loop means that one part of your dissociated awareness (the "Witness") must recognize when the other part of your dissociated awareness (the "Monkey")[23] moves away from repetition of the loop and becomes involved in other inner attracting experiences. The "Witness"—if it can enable some part of critical judgment—can bring the "Monkey" back to repetition. Because the "Witness" always brings the "Monkey" back to the repetition, this constitutes another cognitive loop and creates a second trance. This specific action sets up a secondary trance loop and such double trances would be typically characteristic of an addictive trance form, if the secondary loop were hypnotic.[24] This internal double trance form creates a stable trance and enhances the trance wyrd.

---

[23] The terms Witness and Monkey are only used here to denote the two separate parts of the dissociated consciousness. These terms have also been used by yogis to describe the same or similar aspects of the mind during meditation, but the nominative terms as used here are not intended to have any particular religious meaning or content.

[24] Because the loops discussed here are internal, they are not of the addictive form. If the secondary loop were external, it would be hypnotic and the combined internal and external loops would constitute the addictive form. Playing music while meditating is also hypnotic.

Starting a Meditation

Sit comfortably but not too comfortably. It does not help to sit in a position in which you will eventually become restlessly uncomfortable, injured, disturbed, or pained.[25] At the same time, it is not helpful to be in a position that induces or promotes sleep or unconsciousness. The posture you pick for meditation influences which cognitive functions become disabled first. If your posture is too comfortable, too relaxing, you might fall into unconscious sleep. Meditation requires your undistracted attention, and so your attention must be maintainable.

During the Meditation

During any meditation you are bound to have unusual thoughts. These thoughts actually occur while you are in a trance. In fact, any thoughts at all, including the cognitive elements of the trance generating loop, occur within a trance. Because short term memory fails in a trance, you might forget to repeat the mantra or forget what you are doing. As soon as you are aware or remember that you are not on the business of the trance generating loop, then you must very gently return to the cognitive elements of the trance generating loop. What is very important is that you do not try to concentrate or force the mind in any way. Because trance is a subtle process, it is critical that what you do in your head must also be very, very gentle and subtle. Generally, the approach is to have the attention on the content of the trance generating loop, over and over again, to experience the most subtle and fine sensations or meanings from this content. If you were touching a rabbit or silk, you might become aware of finer and finer textures, even energies or sensations of intelligence and life. It is this very gentle and

---

[25] Fakirs may use a bed of nails in order to produce a bodily pain from which meditation will provide an anesthesia. Because of the external aspect of the secondary loop—bodily pain—it has the characteristics of an addictive trance. Fakirs use pain in the "Witness" to force a more regular loop in the "Monkey." This does produce a stronger wyrd, but at the expense of general body awareness. One can argue that such addictive trances in which body awareness becomes less do not lead to a true enlightenment, but rather increases the dark powers.

subtle action of attention that promotes the best effects of meditation. The content itself can be so subtle that it disappears entirely.

If there are external noises such as loud bangs, the telephone ringing, doors slamming, dogs barking, guns firing, cars crashing, people shrieking, children crying, lovers quarreling, and bombs falling, you must simply let your attention be on the cognitive elements of the trance generating loop without trying to influence, become curious about, or trying to avoid the external noises. These noises are part of life. Yet, the subtleties of meditation become much sweeter and delicate if there were no such interruptions. So, if you can manage to meditate in a quiet and peaceful place such as a cemetery, a cave, under the ocean, in an abandoned mine, in an isolated park, on a mountain top, or even on a distant planet, so much the better for your meditation results. But short of those ideals, you will need let the external noises occur as they do.

Ending the Meditation

Bringing a meditation to an end means first that you stop the trance generating loop: stop repeating the mantra and stop all cognitive loops. But this is not enough.

In spite of the fact that you stop the trance generating loop, the trance will persist for a good while—some minutes, hours or even days, if you meditate for many hours. So, after you stop the trance generating loop, just sit quietly for a few minutes with your eyes closed. Then open your eyes and look around for a few seconds. If you open only one eye, the trance tends not to be interrupted. Then ground yourself. This means to touch your head to the earth, or to get your head wet (splash water on your face). Make a loud noise, ring a bell, bang a gong, or clap. The subtle effects of trance are usually broken with mild shocks; this means that firing a gun or artillery shell is not usually necessary to break a trance.

There are some alternate trance generating loops on the physical level that can alter your meditation trance or may replace it.

If you do some yoga or some jogging or some swimming after meditation, you may only succeed in starting other different trances. Be aware that to stop a trance you must stop the loop that generates the trance, but if you start other loops, you will start other trances. In order to prevent the effect of confusion, stop one trance before starting another.[26]

Needless to say, avoid television before, during, and after meditation. It is no help at all.

Avoid other potentially addictive behaviors as well, unless you wish to create strong trance wyrds over which you may have no control. Specifically, I mean, don't drink or use drugs with meditation.

Effects You can Expect

Generally you can expect deep relaxation and increased alertness. Meditation lowers blood pressure and generally promotes a healthy nervous system. However, you can also expect some cognitive functions to remain quiescent for a variable period of time after the trance generating loop has stopped. This is a normal effect of meditation, and it is helpful to be aware of it. You may, in fact, have less body awareness. You may have disabled some short term memory functions and therefore forget whatever it was that was bothering you. Your critical judgment may be disabled for a period of time and your feeling of inner peace might allow you to become persuaded more easily. Likewise, your volition may be disabled and you may prefer to sit and relax rather than do anything. Literalism will be increased. These are all normal short-term effects of meditation, but long-term meditation will increase and stabilize these effects. The effect of the increase in literalism, for example, makes a person seem "spacey" as they don't seem to make the normal "connections." Persons who practice meditation, without knowing what they are doing, can be forgetful, lack motivation,

---

[26] Gurus will insist that a prospective disciple completely abandon prior teachers and teachings before accepting them.

can be unable to reason or understand causation (cause and effect) and are excessively literal—in other words, "space cases." Their symptoms are due to a lack of proper termination of trance. Indeed, they might not even know or remember what they were mentally repeating to produce the trance.

Difficulties in Meditation

If you have difficulty in meditation, here are some ways to overcome those difficulties.

First, make sure you start correctly according to whichever type of meditation you practice. Specific physical positions do influence which cognitive functions become disabled first.

Second, don't have any expectations. An expectation is "future pacing" and requires enhanced inner mental imagery. You can think of this as another trance. It will interfere with your meditation.

Third, as you meditate, it is quite likely that you will experience disabled cognitive functions, and these will result in boredom, forgetting what you are doing, being unable to decide, tunnel vision, and so on. This is normal. These are indicators that you are meditating correctly up to that point. When in these disabled cognitive states, restart or continue your meditation. This makes a second trance and helps to stabilize the first trance.

Fourth, disturbing thoughts, no matter what they are, need to be passively ignored. Stay with your meditation.

Fifth, terminate your meditation properly.

These guidelines will solve most difficulties in meditation.

Because critical judgment is suspended during a meditation trance, outside influences can have a powerful effect on you. Reducing the possibility of outside influences can only aid meditation.

Making Suggestions

Meditation opens one to the influence of suggestion because of the suspension of critical judgment and other cognitive functions. Making suggestions to yourself, mentally, or allowing a meditation leader (guru?) to speak to you while you are open and uncritical may be acceptable for some people. But unless such gurus are skilled in hypnotic suggestion techniques and have been proven to have no nefarious or hidden agendas, a wise path for yourself would be to avoid situations in which anyone speaks or attempts suggestions either during or after your meditation period. Resist the attraction you might have to allow someone else to suggest that you go deeper into a meditation trance. That is hypnosis; you would open an uncritical channel by allowing anyone to make verbal suggestions during your meditation. "Let go and let God" is a particularly vicious form of trance abuse, leading to victimization and exploitation by cult leaders.[27] The problem with this particular "mantra" is that it is so non-specific that it encourages abandonment of personal responsibility. For example, why not just close your eyes, walk across the freeway at night? "Let go and let God." Why not consume that fifth of whiskey before driving across country? Why not take a sexual risk with someone you know is infectious? Why not let your pastor or preacher tell you how to run your life? "Let go and let God" is so vague it opens a suggestible person to a Pandora's Box of dangers.

Practical Meditation: Mantra

Inducing a meditation trance is something you must do yourself. That is, the limitation of attention and the repetition of a sequence (it need not be a mantra) are the only critical conditions. What is important is to be able to distinguish between a meditation trance—which is a technique you do yourself, and a hypnotic trance—which is a technique someone does for you or to you.

Autogenic training or self-hypnosis in which the primary responsibility remains with the solitary practitioner is probably a safer way to induce a meditation trance than allowing a medita-

---

[27]The unspoken assumption is that the hypnotist (priest) is or becomes the interpreter of God or God's Word. Be careful.

tion guide induce a hypnotic trance as a guided meditation. When groups of practitioners of meditation come together to enjoy a group meditation, one should be alert of the potential for a meditation trance to basically degrade into a hypnotic trance, and with the concomitant possibilities of trance abuse taking place.

One specific technique for meditation trance induction goes like this: Use the mantra Shirim. Close your eyes, wait about a half a minute, and then start silently repeating the mantra over and over again. Eventually you will become bored and may even forget to repeat the mantra. This means that the residual awareness in the dissociated plane is of a higher energy than the trance generating loop which consists of the mantra. This is normal and simply means you are going into a trance. When you are aware that you have forgotten to repeat the mantra, immediately go back to the mantra. This sets up a secondary trance generating loop from your dissociated state back to the primary trance generating loop (the mantra).

Another important point is to "remember" the mantra rather than mentally repeating it clearly. Remembering the mantra invokes the residual awareness component, and this will help you to remain in the dissociated trance plane. Hearing the mantra faintly is also a technique for retaining the dissociative state.

Thoughts which occur do so while you are in a dissociated state. Never think you are "just thinking" or that your consciousness is "normal." It's not. You are dissociated, and therefore some of your cognitive faculties are disabled.

Mantras are not the only vehicles for inducing a meditation trance. However, if you would like a list of mantras to use, you can use any of the following short list, but there are many, many more from the religious and nonreligious traditions of the world:

Eng, Em, Enga, Aing, Aim, Ainga, Aima, Shiring, Shirim, Hiring, Hirim, Kiring, Kirim, Sham, Shama, Ing, Im, Shiama, Om Mane Padme Hum, Ya Ali, Hu, Hare Kali Om, Jai Ram, Hare Om, Om Nama Shivaya, Yaweh, Shri Shri Aing Aing Namah Namah, Money, Love, Sex, Health, Happiness, Power, Peace, Allah Hu.

Practical Meditation: Using the Breath

Besides using any of the five senses as vehicles for the trance generating loop, you can also use somatic awareness such as watching your own breath. This technique is popular among Buddhists, for example. Again, the trance generating loop is the breath itself: the inhalation, the retention, the exhalation. The dissociated trance plane occurs when you forget to watch your breath. Then you should gently remember to watch your breathing. This will establish the secondary trance generating loop.

Breathing suffuses oxygen throughout your body and eliminates carbon dioxide (CO_2) from it. Hence, inhalation and exhalation exchanges should have equal volumes of gas.

Practical Meditation: Using Visualization

Other meditation techniques, such as visualization, will be effective, as well. You can actively visualize a face or a symbol (a circle, a cross, a star, the number nine, the mantra Hu), and when the symbol fades and you become aware that it has faded, you reconstruct it again mentally. This is basically of the same form as the technique described earlier above using mantras or watching your breath. Again, the trance generating loop does not need to be a mantra or a visualization and the actual content of the loop does not need to be religious. It also can even be political, emotional, or financial.

Elaborate mental visualizations can be constructed to create trance. For example, you might imagine a vivid jungle scene with a stream nearby, and a small cottage in which lives a wise old man[28] who invites you to sit outside while you ask him various questions. This visualization can be a ritual in which there is a repetition of the entire image and action within that image. The repetition itself creates the trance. The content modifies the cognitive functions by acting as a subtle suggestion within

---

[28] Some traditions suggest that no person be visualized in order to prevent exploitation by cultists. I am highly suspicious of any visualization technique promoted by a group in which a specific guru, holy man, or teacher is visualized.

the trance. To explain further so you get the idea: A stream of water will be cooling and purifying so you can forget your guilt or problems. A cottage will be warm and comforting so you can relax. The wise old man is an authority figure who tells you what to do so you can trust and follow. Although these implied images need not be explicitly made, they unfold themselves while you meditate and they have an effect on what kinds of images your mind will create for you.

Mandalas

As for the use of mandalas—whether Tibetan, Mayan, or Sufi—in contemplation or meditation the same trance analysis applies. The repetition creates a dissociated trance plane and consequent disabling of some cognitive functions. This also would be classified as a hypnotic trance since part of the loop is "outside." It is only when the entire loop is "inside" that it is a meditation trance. However, some mandalas are only used as teaching aid. During the teaching process, the type of trance is hypnotic. But, after the student knows and has a vivid image of what the mandala looks like, then it may be visualized internally. Then it is a meditation trance and no longer a hypnotic trance. Different traditions have different techniques.

Practical Meditation: Movement of Awareness

Other meditation trance techniques involve what might be called "movement of awareness" where you place your inner awareness on the chakras[29] and move this awareness from chakra to chakra. As you do this, you can associate with each chakra, a mantra, a color, a smell, and so on.[30] You may integrate a particular body movement with your inner awareness as your awareness moves along your spine or—using visualization—throughout the far reaches of the cosmos. Elaborate meditation trance techniques such as these are popular among the Tibetans and Sufis and

---

[29] A chakra is a center of energy in the body.
[30] Combining different sense "modalities" is a way of deepening a trance.

were practiced by ancient civilizations as well. Again, the trance generating loop in this technique consists of each point of your awareness. The content is not so important for the creation of the trance, but the fact that the content is repeated is critical. What is important about content is to realize that when the dissociation occurs, the content will then act as a suggestion. The suggestion need not be verbal—it can be visual, sensory—but when it is repeated often enough for long periods of time it will potentiate the trance wyrd.

One meditation technique is to place Om at the crown of the head, then move your awareness to the space between your eyebrows and place Na there. Then move your awareness to your throat and place Ma there. Then move your awareness to your heart area and place Shi there. Then move your awareness to just below your belly button and place Va there. Then move your awareness to your genitals and place Ya there. Then move your awareness to your anal area and place Om there. If you have a mala of beads, it is good to count one bead. For beginners, this takes some effort because the trance tends to break. Then, move your awareness rather rapidly and lightly backwards, touching the points in the reverse direction: Om, Ya, Va, Shi, Ma, Na, and Om. Rest there for a second and start over again.

Another meditation involves imagining a light blue rain falling on you and washing all sorts of impurities and disease out of your body, mind, and soul back into the earth.[31] There are many other variations.

Practical meditation: The Pentagram

A final form of meditation involving the movement of consciousness is done with the form of a pentagram (a five pointed star). The pentagram is an ancient symbol.[32] It has been associated with pagans, Christians, Ishtar, Satan (only since mid 20th century), witches, the planet Venus, and the mathematical

---

[31] This is a purported Egyptian sufi meditation technique from J. G. Bennett.
[32] The pentagram has been used at least since 3500 BCE.

value for the Golden Mean, Phi or ϕ. One form of the meditation is done as follows:

First, place your awareness at the crown of your head, and then move your awareness to your left foot. Then from your left foot move your awareness to your right hand. From there move your awareness to your left hand. Then from your left hand move your awareness to your right foot. Finally, move your awareness to the crown of your head. If you are standing, with your legs apart and your hands outstretched to your sides, shoulder height, you will have made the form of a pentagram. Make the corners sharp; at least don't cut corners. This entire movement is one loop. It will create a trance after a few repetitions.

Secondly, as you do this loop, you will probably space out or lose track of where you are. This is because you are dissociated and thus short term memory as well as critical judgment fail. As soon as you realize that you have lost it, or spaced out, then go back to the first loop. This makes the second loop of this practice, connecting the result of the trance with the cause.

Thirdly, as you discover the effects of this meditation, connect the effects of the first two loops with the first inner loop. This will constitute a third loop and will increase the wyrd considerably if you persist in doing this meditation every day for some weeks.

There are many variations possible with this meditation, including changing the size of the pentagram, associating each point with an energy, and so on.

An appreciation of Hermetic philosophical principles may lead you to contemplate how this pentagram meditation is connected to universal consciousness.

Practical Meditation: Ritual Combinations

Effective ritual begins with establishing a trance. Whatever the ritual intent is, trance creates the cognitive functions needed for effective practice and disables those cognitive functions that interfere with ritual purposes.

In a sense, meditation is a magical act that must be done many times to increase the wyrd. In addition, just as practice is needed to see while in a trance, to hear while in a trance, to think while in a trance, and to perceive clearly while in a trance, practice is needed to move while in a trance, to draw a magic circle while in a trance, to chant while in a trance, and to banish and invoke while in a trance. This is how ritual is made effective.

In the movement of awareness, an attempt is made to move a bead while in a somewhat complicated trance generating loop. This simple act itself for beginners is nearly impossible to do without breaking the trance. Practice makes it easier. Ritual combinations takes it a giant step further. Ritual combinations require that complicated sequences of physical action take place while one is entirely in trance. Considerable skill in trance is needed to accomplish this.

Nevertheless, one first meditates for some time in order to establish a deep trance. While in the trance, one can perform an established ritual involving movement, and perhaps chanting as well. Because of the nature of trance, the subjective reality will appear different to a greater or lesser degree than the ordinary reality. You can, of course, dance while in a trance. Some trance dancers toss the head back as a trigger to induce a trance.

As in all ritual combinations of trance, a subtle balance must be maintained in order for the trance not to be broken during the physical activity of the ritual. This balance will allow for the accumulation of trance wyrd energies.

Strong trance wyrds often do not subjectively feel strong. It is something like being in a speeding jet plane: one is not particularly aware of the high speed at which one is traveling. Likewise, strong trance wyrds manifest as a change in internal reality, which appears perfectly normal. Strong trance wyrds can be more easily detected by those who are not in a trance and who watch you perform the ritual; it sometimes happens that there are unusual visual or other effects.

If you are a witch, magician, or priest, and you wish to make an effective ritual, every act must be done at least three times, preferably seven times. For example, drawing the magic circle should be done seven times. Banishing should be done seven times; invoking requires seven times, etc. If only done once, what distinguishes a magical act from an ordinary act? Repetition will increase the trance wyrd substantially, so repetition is essential for any ritual.

At the conclusion of a ritual there must be an absolute, resolute, and definite end to the ritual, as well as to the trance, which essentially means terminating all trance generating loops. Grounding and reestablishing the prior state of consciousness is another form of balance which releases the trance wyrd in an effective way.

Failing to release the trance wyrd can result in trancelings and apparently compulsive and pathological behaviors or other addictive effects. Such uncontrolled trancelings left ungrounded are not pleasant and hence result in an impoverished condition. To be sure, ungrounded trancelings might make you feel high or trippy and spaced out, but they interfere with efficiency, cause mistakes and big problems. Grounding trancelings will distinguish the magician from the fool.

Mixed Forms of Meditation

Most practical forms of meditation are actually multiple loops, that is, they are complex meditation trance forms. So, for example, you start with a single mental loop. When that trance has started, you start another loop—perhaps a visualization. Then, for each element of the visualization, you mentally start another meditation loop at each chakra. Additionally, the loops that are used to deepen a trance actually make the trance more complex. As you will see later, these complex forms can also become hypnotic and addictive trance forms.

By now you should have the feeling that although the model for trance is rather simple, the practical implications are rather vast. The other important fact is that meditating takes time. You have to actually sit down and do a practice, sometimes for years, in order to reap the benefits or to figure out what the actual effects are. There are many reasons not to meditate. One big reason is the resistance your own mind will naturally create. There is not enough time; the phone is ringing; I have a screaming child; I need to work; and so on. Meditation can be a powerfully boring experience, or it can be a rich source of mental distraction by creating irritating thoughts that work to discourage all but the most determined meditator. Also, there are thousands of forms of meditation and limited time for practicing every one of them, so which particular form of meditation will be the most efficient for you? In addition, of the thousands of forms of meditation, some forms are potentially dangerous or can produce only confusion and delusion. How does the unenlightened mind discriminate between the forms that produce the results you want from the forms that produce no good end?

You must look for the effects of meditation in your daily life, not necessarily during the time that you are meditating. Also, effects can be very subtle.

Exercises

1. Daydream trances consist of trance generating loops in which the cognitive objects are feelings. Using in turn, the emotions of love, hope, and fear, invent three different trance generating loops using images or memories from your own life, and practice each one for a maximum of ten minutes on three separate days. Record your experiences.

2. Use the traditional Om Nama Shivaya Om but imagine placing each syllable on a chakra. Om is at the top of the head; Na at the space between the eyebrows; Ma at the throat; Shi at the heart; Va at the navel; Ya at the genitals; Om at the space between the genitals and the anus. Then repeat it backwards, moving your awareness back to the top of your head. This counts as one repetition. Do this 108 times. What did you notice?

3. Using your experience from Exercise 2, take one deep breath at each chakra so that your exhalation ends when your consciousness is still fixed on the chakra. Again, what did you notice?

4. Using your experience from Exercise 2, and holding a mala[33] of 108 beads, count one bead for each full repetition. Do this 108 times. What did you notice?
5. What are the effects of the pentagram meditation? Does it affect your dream awareness for example? Is this effect related to the sharpness of the points of the pentagram? Why or why not?

Questions

1. Explain the "relaxation response" with trance theory.
2. Pick any complex Tibetan meditation practice and identify the loops. How does each identified loop affect the trance wyrd?

---

[33] A mala is a traditional Indian rosary, usually consisting of rudraksh seeds (for men) or sandalwood beads (for women).

Hypnosis

Do You Need a Guide?

A Definition of Hypnosis

A hypnotic trance is a trance consisting of two trance generating loops (TGL). In the first loop, part of the content is external to the person being hypnotized. This is the loop typically controlled by the hypnotist. The content of the second loop is internal to the person being hypnotized. This second TGL produces a meditation trance. These two loops together constitute the simplest form of hypnotic trance.

Hypnotic trances with multiple internal or external loops are complex hypnotic trances. If one or more of the internal meditation loops is connected with the content of the first loop, the trance will be strengthened. A hypnotist will try to create a complex hypnotic trance because the goal, generally, is to create a strong hypnotic trance. Practically, the way a hypnotist will do this is with metaphorical allusion, that is with words that internally engage the person being hypnotized.

Deep or strong hypnotic trances always have tertiary loops that help turn the hypnotic trance into an addictive trance. These forms of deep hypnotic trance, like an addictive trance, are associated with compulsive behaviors and personality disorders.

The distinguishing characteristic of hypnosis is that one of the cognitive loops is external. If this external loop exists, then the trance is hypnotic, by definition. All forms of trance, as I have indicated earlier, are created by a cognitive loop, and every repeated cognitive loop will eventually produce a trance. A trance is a form of dissociation in which a variety of specific cognitive functions are disabled or altered. The specific set of affected cognitive functions and the order in which they become disabled or altered determine the "flavor" of the trance—whether it is deep, light, etc.

The most important cognitive function to be disabled for hypnosis to occur is critical judgment. Once critical judgment is disabled, one becomes suggestible. There are many ways to disable critical judgment and the repetition of a cognitive loop is only one of the ways. If your attention is diverted or fascinated by anything, or involved in a memory, fear, or fantasy, then your critical judgment is probably disabled—just enough for you to become suggestible. In a later chapter, I will discuss electronic, microwave, and ultrasonic forms of hypnotic trance induction which simply bypass your critical judgment since you cannot even hear the suggestions.

The defining characteristic of a meditation trance is that you create the trance loop and it stays inside your own mind. This is different from a hypnotic trance. The defining characteristic of a hypnotic trance is that a hypnotist creates an external trance loop that supports the creation of an internal trance loop. Both loops together create the condition for a hypnotic trance to occur.

In the prior chapter we learned that with meditation, the cognitive loop remains wholly in your mind. But with hypnosis a part of that loop is outside of your mind. And usually the hypnotist is providing the content of that loop in the form of words, rhythms, or images. The part of the loop, which is in your mind, is often a meditative form, especially when you dissociate. No one usually knows what the content of the meditation loop is—not even the hypnotist. The content may be suggested, of course, but the subject may really be internally involved in repeated fantasies of some sort to block out the hypnotist. This blocking will heighten suggestibility and make hypnotic commands more effective.

Hypnosis is quite common, according this definition. If someone sings a song to you—and repeats it—the song can become part of an external cognitive loop creating a hypnotic trance. Lullabies are hypnotic for this reason. So are religious chants. The sing-song of a salesman will become hypnotic, as well, if repeated enough.

To be more specific, what is done in order to produce basic hypnosis is to first start with a simple cognitive loop, that is, a repeating set of words, sounds, feelings, or images. It can also be what hypnotists call the "hypnotic voice," a soothing, monotonous, sing-song, rhythmical way of delivering a command such as "You are feeling very relaxed and sleepy," for example. Certain types of preachers have developed this way of speaking. Some politicians have also perfected the hypnotic voice. And, of course, master salesmen, hustlers, con artists, flim-flam men, gypsies, and many others—including hypnotists—all use the hypnotic voice.

The hypnotic voice sets up a rhythm that is more or less content free.[34] That is, it need not have any specific commands, but it is the repetition itself causing the trance. Repeated commands given without the hypnotic voice will also induce a hypnotic trance. So, technically, when a hypnotic voice is combined with repeated commands, you have two cognitive loops, each of which produces a trance. The rhythmic crashing of waves on the shore, the chirping of birds, etc., also produce a hypnotic trance. However, as you have learned from earlier chapters, trances are additive, so when you have two trances, the trance wyrd becomes much stronger.

The content of commands—such as "You cannot feel your right arm"—creates specific effects. The first few times it is repeated, the subject may mentally criticize or block it.[35] However, if the repetition continues for some time, the subject will start a trance. The trance will be felt subjectively as boredom or even anger. But the effect is the same. A light, dissociated condition occurs in which the subject's awareness seems normal, but which has a disabled cognitive function—that of critical judgment. The disabling of critical judgment means that little or no critical attention is paid to the content of a command.

---

[34] Because a trance is started by repetition alone, even a ticking clock, which has no command content, can induce a hypnotic trance.

[35] This has the same effect as creating a taboo, that is, a secret covering.

When critical judgment is disabled, that and that alone produces "suggestibility."

Another effective way to disable critical judgment is through shock or fear. Fear sets into motion a fight or flight response and an internal dialogue as to what to do next. Flight or fight? Maybe there is nothing you can do, and in this helpless state your critical judgment simply does not work any more. Then the person making the threat can give you a command such as "Put your hands up and turn around!" or "Give me your wallet!" or "Obey your Leader!" and doubtless you will comply.

More subtle or continuous threats or uncertainties can have the effect of decreasing communication, social cohesion, and cooperation, as a defense against fear. What happens? First, paranoia and suspicion cause a decrease in social communication—because of the doubt of who might be trustworthy. And then an increase in anger, despair, and cynicism results. Secondly, fantasies having violent content increase. Sometimes, the violent fantasies are acted upon. Thirdly, social or "tribal" defense systems begin to form. These may manifest as militias, mutual defense groups, or other types of militarized or political resistance. Finally, fear either continues to perpetuate itself or people rediscover a common humanity in which love vanquishes fear, and critical judgment becomes re-enabled.

Creating an Hypnotic Trance

Repetition is the key. Repeat suggestions and then test them. Then add additional trance inducing loops with more suggestions and then test them. Each suggestion should ask for more cooperation while adding to the loops that have already started. Think of building a structure with loops and making each loop stronger and stronger. It is important to make secondary loops in order to increase the wyrd, which at the same time disables various cognitive functions. For example, a suggestion like "Whenever you want to move your arm, you cannot," sets up a secondary loop which—over the long term—increases the wyrd. Whenever a hypnotist can create intense inner involvement with complex trance inducing loops, the resulting hypnotic trance will be deep and successful.

The Disabled Cognitive Functions

With respect to hypnotic trances, the first disabled cognitive function seems to be the ego. That is, the subjective feeling is that one becomes a witness to the hypnosis. That is already a trance, but the trance needs to become deeper. A second common subjective sensation is that one feels bored, especially when there is much repetition. At some point in time, after being a witness and being bored for awhile, one can easily become involved in one's inner state or involved with an internal fantasy of some sort. Why not? And how much easier it is when you even have both the encouragement and permission of the hypnotist? Why not just ignore the hypnotist altogether and get involved with that inner fantasy?

The next thing which happens is that you forget what you were doing or how you got there. It is your short term memory failing. It doesn't matter to you because you still have your inner fantasy. After that, your critical judgment becomes wobbly, becomes suspended, and that doesn't matter either because you can just listen to the hypnotist or not. He'll take care of every-thing . . . and there you are—in a trance.

You might also feel a narrowing of awareness as though you were entering a tunnel. Some people feel a kind of pressure, a binding, a restraint of some sort. If you trust the hypnotist, this feeling can be quite comfortable and reassuring, allowing you to go even deeper into a trance.

You are conscious, of course, and it seems that you are in your right mind. But, unfortunately, that is not true. You are in one or more trances, and the hypnotist merely has to make the sugges-tion that you are stuck in the trance and that any effort to get out of the trance only leads you deeper. This is a tertiary trance loop that increases the trance depth and the wyrd trance force.

Increasing the tension or emotional involvement through fear or pain or disgust will also deepen the hypnotic trance. The subject may want to escape but cannot, and thus the subject actually prefers to go even deeper into trance and "ignore" the hypnotist. This also sets up the tertiary loop in which the more you want to stop, the less you are able, and the more you go deeper into trance.

Some hypnotic strategies use disgust or humor to engage the inner critic. The more disgusting or funny or immoral the words or acts of the hypnotist are, the more you think that he is an idiot. And yet, you continue in your trance, you do not stop him, you do not complain, and you ignore him. Importantly, you do not break the trance or resist in any way. Maybe you even think that he is funny. Your cynical attitude merely plays into the trance deepening process. Has this ever happened to you? It is a common technique used by salesmen, con-artists, politicians, and even priests. You might even think that the hypnotist has a sort of charisma. Yet, if you analyze the trance, you can discover that he repeatedly encourages inner involvement and suspension of critical judgment—essentially the conditions for a trance.

The Wyrd

A hypnotic trance becomes a strong trance when there are multiple trance generating loops. That is, multiple loops create multiple trance wyrds, which are additive in effect. The sum effect of multiple wyrds is a stronger trance.

This means that if a hypnotist uses only one type of loop, the trance produced will be very light and easily broken. Generally, hypnotic trances consist of multiple trance generating loops in order to produce a strong or deep trance. However, simple one loop trances are easy to create and can also be effective carriers of suggestion with the right subject.

In Neuro-Linguistic Programming or NLP, hypnotherapists speak of "different modalities," that is, using words associated with different physical senses. They assert that it is the simultaneous use of different modalities that produces strong trance. The Trance Model makes the analysis somewhat differently.

Each modality or sense has a strong cohesiveness of association. The associative contents of each sense do not overlap except metaphorically. So, when different senses are used simultaneously the cohesiveness of association is lowered dramatically resulting in an increase in the wyrd. When a loop is used in that context, a trance is certain to result.

Extending this idea further, using words associated with trance—trigger words, for example, or any words which invoke different cognitive functions—will result in a stronger wyrd. If I write a hypnotic script using memory, sensory stimulation, and arithmetic processing, I will certainly create a strong hypnotic trance. For example, I might say, "As you remember to listen to my voice, you will feel more and more relaxed as I count forward from a hundred to one." If I repeated that phrase a hundred times, you doubtless would have a compulsive feeling of relaxation. But if I calculate the wyrd of that formula, I must also take into consideration the wyrd components of the individual words: remember, listen, feel, count, and the arithmetic processing of 100, 99, 98, 96, 25, 14, 79, and so on. In addition, the contradictory statement of counting "forward" instead of "backward" requires a suspension of critical judgment in order for it to make sense. The use of contradictions and illogic in hypnotic scripting also increases the wyrd—by intent. So, the way to induce hypnotic trance is to choose content that increases the wyrd while employing repetition of cognitive objects.

For example, a hypnotist might refer to "that terrible accident" or that time "the criminal put a pun[36] to your head" or "when you imagine him raping you over and over" these repeated images stimulate curiosity, incredulity, fear, and disgust, but repeating such highly connotative and fearful images helps to drive the listener into a deep trance. Television images also are used in the same way. It is like the enchantment of a black magician. With time, whenever such images are used as triggers, a trance results enabling uncritical acceptance of limited choices. You may easily find examples of this: "9-11,

---

[36] "pun" not "gun," which causes additional cognitive overload.

9-11, 9-11! Terrorist! Terrorist! Terrorist!" There. I'll bet you're feeling better already knowing how easy it is to put you into a trance. Find some more examples in your life and discover the loops, the taboos, and the disabled cognitive functions, and you will begin to end the enchantment.

Disabling Critical Judgment

If you are a hypnotist, you will want to disable critical judgment as soon and as rapidly as possible so that your client or target will not be able to critically think about the nonsense you are feeding them. One way to do this is to make very long sentences—with embedded commands—connected by words such as "and," "while," "because," "as you," etc. It is not necessary that each part of the sentence make any sense whatsoever in relation to other parts of the sentence. Why? Because you want your client or target to get overwhelmed by trying to make sense of your sentence and to finally give up, that is, to disable his or her critical judgment so that he or she becomes suggestible like a good hypnotic subject. In other words, you must talk sympathetically, but almost like an idiot, a psychotic, or a pathetic fool. People will need to suspend their critical judgment to try to figure out what the hell you are babbling about. Panhandlers, shysters, con-artists, criminals, and presidents have successfully used this specific hypnotic technique. Technically, what is being done is to create a cognitive object system with low cohesiveness of association so that critical judgment is defeated. And then to strengthen the total trance wyrd by creating multiple trances using multiple loops (repetition). Done in a subtle, artistic manner, this method of hypnotic induction is powerful, irresistible, and seductive.

Trigger Words

There are some words that have a relatively low cohesiveness of association. That is, if I asked you what does "mother" mean to you, you might need to think for several seconds before you answered.

If I asked you about some other words, such as "shoe," "apple," or "sunshine" it might take you less time than for "mother." A low cohesiveness of association is reflected in the high response delay time for any word. That is, if a word has very few associations, is not abstract or emotionally charged, then it means perhaps one specific thing and not several. It takes us fewer seconds to come up with a "meaning," so it has a high cohesiveness of association. It might not matter how frequently that word repeats in our consciousness, or is associated with other words.

There are many other words that have a relatively higher response delay, such as "remember," "imagine," "special," "deserve," "long ago," etc. These words have a longer association delay than other words. Some words have a special meaning but are still non-specific enough so that the association delay tends to be longer. Such words as "freedom," "democracy," "terrorist," "love," and "patriot" come to mind. These words have a low cohesiveness of association and nearly always result in a higher associative response delay time. When these words are used by a hypnotist, the subject tends to space out in trying to imagine what on earth the hypnotist could mean. Spacing out means suspending critical judgment, thinking metaphorically, or engaging inner involvement just enough so that you become a little more suggestible. Then, Gotcha! A hypnotist can take advantage of this brief second that you are spaced out and weave in a command or enhance the dissociation with a loop.

The high associative delay words that cause dissociation could be called "trigger" words, but they are not exactly the same as the trained signal words a hypnotist might use to invoke a trance. However, the theoretical structure is the same in the sense that, when used, they increase the wyrd.

A trance is created by cognitive loops, not trigger words. But a trance can be associated with a touch, pressure, or word and it is this association a hypnotist calls a trigger. The idea is that if the trigger is invoked then the underlying cognitive loop and trance will also be recreated. When trained and tested, such association triggers may be used to invoke the loops that result in a prior established trance.

Dennis R. Wier

A trigger word also invokes a high associative response delay and has a low cohesiveness of association, and some of the specific internal associations form the cognitive loops that result in a trance being created. Using triggers, however, can possibly create many uncontrolled trances including trancelings and unhinged trances.

"Trigger words" can also mean words or signals used by a hypnotist to train a hypnotic subject. There is nothing magical about trigger words except perhaps that when repeated they create a higher wyrd than do other, more normal words.

Embedded Commands

An embedded command is a phrase or sentence that has an explicit but unremarked command in it. For example, the question: "Would you drink a coffee with me?" contains "drink a coffee with me" as a command. This construction is effective as a command or suggestion only if critical judgment is disabled. Many innocent sounding invitations and seeming harmless choices may contain embedded commands by willful design of a hypnotist. When combined with words with low cohesiveness of association, critical judgment can be side-stepped and the embedded commands accepted.

"Can you remember how good it felt when you kissed the one you loved close that warm night long ago and the feelings you had as you go to sleep in that dreamy way, relaxed now, and staying open, and wanting it all over again, now . . ."

These sorts of scripts are very easy to write. They combine low cohesiveness of association words such as remember, good, feel, kiss, love, etc., with run-on sentences connected with words such as: as, while, and, because, and embedded commands: remember, go to sleep, relaxed, wanting it, now.

Who Uses Hypnosis?

It would be nice if only cowboys with white hats used hypnotic techniques, but, in fact, hypnosis is used by all sorts of people.

Authorities of all sorts are in a dominant position, which causes suspension of critical judgment. Any authority can make hypnotic errors or inadvertently use bad trance engineering and get the opposite results of what they intend.

Some medical professionals know that the patient can heal his or her self. Placebos sometimes work more effectively than more traditional medicines. So, trained medical professionals can help your body heal quicker with some gentle hypnosis. But such hypnosis needs to be done subtly in such a way that critical judgment is not awakened. Embedded commands are most often used by doctors and nurses, but this can also backfire and inhibit healing.

Psychologists, psychiatrists, social workers and many other people-helpers will use hypnosis if they can encourage a client to act in a way which benefits themselves or which reduces harm.

Religious folks also use hypnosis. Generally, hypnosis might be used to promote a specific belief, but it can also be used to compel obedience to religious precepts or to encourage folks to become more generous, guilty, religious, or devoted. In many cases hypnosis is used to gain converts, to demonstrate magical powers, or to produce healing, and to increase donations. Demonstrating an altered state of consciousness, showing the "divine light" and so on, are also ways hypnosis is used by the religious. In many congregations there is a "feel good" mood-making, which can result in feelings of self-esteem or innate goodness or "blessedness." These feelings—strictly resulting from hypnosis—may cover a multitude of sins, absolve guilt, increase self-esteem, and promote feelings of wholeness. So, it is quite possible for a member of a church to actually be non-compassionate, non-loving, obsessive, greedy, cruel, non-forgiving, a liar to oneself and others, and a secret thief, and yet, wear a permanent smile and feel truly "blessed" and happy, not at all guilty, and "saved." Such is the magic of hypnosis.

Advertisers routinely use hypnotic techniques including repetition and embedded commands in order to create brand loyalty, encourage brand switching, or to change purchase preferences. Images which have nothing to do with a product are often used to hypnotically create favorable associations. That is, critical judgment is by-passed so that a delusional belief, an obsession, or addictive desire is created for a particular product. Automobiles are often sold for delusional feelings of sex and power. Cigarette advertising sells the delusion of immortality in the face of high risk behavior or death. Hidden in the advertisement, of course, is the taboo of feeling powerless, impotence, self-destruction, or death. To fully understand how hypnosis works in these cases, it is very important to expose and consciously understand and express the taboo. Expressing the taboo can "de-fang" the hypnotic wyrd.

Practice of Hypnosis

Professional hypnotherapists often must subscribe to a Code of Professional Ethics. But the existence of a code of ethics does not mean that everyone who uses hypnotic techniques subscribes to those same ethical standards. It is often a tenant of such ethical standards that a hypnotist will not give a client a suggestion that might morally or ethically compromise the client. While this ethical standard is laudable, it falsely implies that hypnosis itself cannot be used by anyone to create compulsions with which a person might disagree with either ethically, morally, or legally. That impression about the technical limits or potential of hypnosis is, unfortunately, misleading. Professional hypnotherapists are the good guys in this case. But there are plenty of people in this world who use hypnosis in unethical ways. Hypnosis itself does not have any built-in ethics.

1-on-1 Mutual Hypnosis

Sometimes it is fun to engage in mutual hypnosis. Mutual hypnosis is done with a partner. There are many forms of mutual hypnosis, but you basically take turns making suggestions. At first, you simply describe your partner. Then they describe you. Then you mix pacing with leading. Allow time for a hypnotic trance to develop. Such mutual hypnosis can be used to explore areas in a relationship not normally possible, or to create fantasies, or to empower each other, or otherwise develop intimate connections and trust.

Although it is fun to create trancelings with mutual hypnosis, make sure you have a way to terminate all the trancelings once you are done playing.

Cults

In general, cults make extensive use of hypnosis. One reason may be the strong desire to have some spiritual experience. Cult members also generally wish to better themselves and in so doing benefit the world. Members of cults often have a desire to do good in the world, but may not know how to do it. Cults often have programs of study and training that purport to bring their members into a deep spiritual brotherhood with the expectation of grace and spiritual experience.

If you join a cult—or you think it might be in a cult—be alert for suggestions that result in your giving up your personal responsibility for yourself. In other words, if you are encouraged or even demanded to follow the leader without critical thinking, or if your critical thinking is turned against you, then you should think seriously about leaving the organization. Cults always ask you to give up your personal responsibility, so that you are more easily controlled. Look for repetitive maxims, chanting, and sing-song simplistic children's songs with embedded commands; these are signs of hypnotic intent.

Hypnosis and Pain

Not many people like pain; most people naturally avoid pain and situations that cause pain. Unavoidable pain will naturally induce a trance. An intense pain sustained for a period of time can drive a person into a deep unconscious trance. Controlling pain means to put one's attention on to something else and to do so repeatedly in such a way that any sensation of pain serves only to put the attention somewhere else. This is a double loop, characteristic of a hypnotic trance.

Let's consider a visit to the dentist and how you might use trance techniques to control pain. If you have any experience with meditation, you already have the main tool. The technique for successful meditation trance uses more than one trance generating loop. If you use a mantra, you know that the second loop is often: "If you stop meditating or forget to meditate, then as soon as you realize that, start the meditation again." For pain, an additional loop is: "As soon as you feel any sensation or pain, start the meditation again." For a dental visit, simply fix your gaze on the ceiling somewhere, meditate including the additional loop. That is, any pain you feel will only serve to make your meditation deeper. You need not try to suggest anything to yourself other than staying with your meditation object or mantra.

The following is a rather long, yet non-exhaustive, list, but it is important for you to understand that hypnotic inductions can occur in a variety of ways. In the following sentences, you can substitute one of your favorite desires—a naughty one to make it interesting—as the [command] in order to understand how trance abuse works in a practical way.

As a variation, the [command] could be a shock or fear producing demand, such as "Put your hands up!" or "Strip!" in order to demonstrate how shock or fear works to disable critical judgment. Where [pace] is indicated, simply describe the person you are talking to in a non-judgmental way, such as "You are sitting there" or "You are smiling now," and so on. Pacing must be non-judgmental because you do not want to excite critical judgment. Where [name] is used in the [command], it is because using the person's name exploits the association to parental or authoritative figures.

Negative suggestions, that is, using "not" in an embedded command context, are sometimes used to impart the positive form of the suggestion. The cohesiveness of association of the words used in embedded commands has an important effect on the effectiveness of the suggestions.

1. [command] in a way that meets your needs.
2. Someone once told me, [command].
3. Someone said, [command].
4. A person could, [name], [command].
5. A person is able to [command].
6. A person may [command], because [any reason].
7. A person may not know if [command].
8. A person might, [name], [command].
9. After [pace] you can [command].
10. All that really matters [command].
11. All that's really important [command].
12. Almost as though [command].
13. And as [pace] occurs, [command] may occur more than you'd expect.
14. And do you notice the beginning of [command]?
15. And if you wish [command].
16. And it appears already that [command].
17. And maybe you'll enjoy noticing [command].
18. And when you [pace], you'll [command].
19. And would you be willing to experience [command]?
20. And would you like to [command]?
21. And you begin to wonder when [command].
22. And you can be pleased [command].
23. And you can wonder [command].
24. And you can wonder what [command].
25. And you will be surprised at [command].
26. And, in an interesting way, you'll discover [command].
27. Are you aware of [command]?
28. As soon as [pace], then [command].
29. As you feel [pace] you recognize [command].
30. Almost as if [command].
31. At first [pace], but later [command].
32. At times like this, some people enjoy [command].
33. Can you [command]?
34. Can you imagine [command]?
35. Can you notice [command]?
36. Can you really enjoy [command]?

37. Do you [command]?
38. Does [command]?
39. Don't [command] too quickly.
40. Don't [command] until you [command].
41. Eventually [command].
42. Everybody [command].
43. Everyone [command].
44. Give yourself the opportunity to see if [command].
45. How would it feel if you [command]?
46. I could tell you that [command] but [command].
47. I don't know if [command].
48. I wonder if you'd like to enjoy [command].
49. I wonder if you'll be pleased to notice [command].
50. I wonder if you'll be reminded [command].
51. I wonder if you've ever noticed [command].
52. I wouldn't tell you to [command], because [pace].
53. I'd like you to begin allowing [command].
54. I'm wondering if [command].
55. I'm wondering if you'll [command], [name] or not.
56. If you [pace], then [command].
57. In all probability [command].
58. In every culture [command].
59. Isn't it important to [command]?
60. It gives everyone a sense of pleasure to [command].
61. It is a very common experience to [command].
62. It isn't necessary to [command].
63. It may be that you'll enjoy [command].
64. It may be that you're already aware of [command].
65. It's easy to [command], is it not?
66. It's so nice to know [command].
67. Just allow it to happen [command].
68. Kind of like [command].
69. Maybe it will surprise you to notice that [command].
70. Maybe you haven't [command], yet.
71. Maybe you'll [command].
72. Most of us [command].
73. Most people [command].

74. One can [name], [command].
75. One could [command], because [pace].
76. One doesn't have to, [name], [command].
77. One may, [name], [command].
78. One might, you know, [command].
79. People can, you know, [command].
80. People don't have to, [name], [command].
81. Perhaps beginning to notice [command].
82. Perhaps noticing [command].
83. Perhaps you are [command].
84. So that it's almost as if [command].
85. Some people [command].
86. Sometime [command].
87. Sooner or later [command].
88. Sooner or later, everyone [command].
89. The closer you get to [command] the more you can [command].
90. The feeling of [pace] will allow you to [command].
91. There was a time when you didn't [command].
92. Try to resist [command].
93. Very likely [command].
94. What happens when you [command]?
95. When you [pace] please [command].
96. When you [pace], then [command].
97. While you [pace] you can [command].
98. Why don't you [command] before you [pace]?
99. Will [command]?
100. Will you [command] now, or will you [command]?
101. Will you [command], or [command], or [command]?
102. With your permission [command].
103. Without knowing it, you've [command].
104. Without really trying, it will just happen all by itself [command].
105. You already know [command].
106. You already know how to [command].
107. You are able to [command].
108. You can [command], because [command].

109. You can [command], can you not?
110. You could [command].
111. You don't have to [command].
112. You don't need to be concerned if [command].
113. You may [command].
114. You may not know if [command].
115. You may or may not [command].
116. You might [command].
117. You might not have noticed [command].
118. You might notice how good [command] feels, when you [command].
119. You might notice the feelings [name] as you [command].
120. You might notice the sensations in [pace] while you [command].
121. You might want to [command], [command] now.
122. You probably already know [command].
123. You won't [command] until [command].
124. You've known all along how to [command].
125. [pace], [pace], [pace], and [command].

Exercises

1. Using one of the embedded command forms above, make a post-hypnotic command and casually repeat it three times to your friend who is watching television.
2. Was it successful?
3. If not, how could it have been made more successful?
4. What does this tell you about trance abuse?
5. With a partner use the hypnotic voice. Observe and describe to them what you see or sense. Repeat the same description and observation multiple times. Connect each description and observation with "and," "while," "because," "as you," etc. It does not need to make sense. Do this for five minutes. Then switch roles. What happens?

6. With a partner use the hypnotic voice. Do the same thing as in the previous exercise. However, after every three observations or descriptions, make a command like "you feel good about yourself," "you feel very relaxed and happy," etc. Then switch roles.
7. Go through an advertisement and underline all of the embedded commands you can find.
8. While watching television news, note images, sounds, or words that stimulate fear or confusion.

Questions

1. How many hours per day do you watch television?
2. What cognitive functions are disabled?
3. What do you do to terminate the trance?
4. What are the potential effects of TV trancelings?
5. Discuss the effect of trance in a democracy.
6. How can a person in a trance, with impaired critical judgment, be expected to make independent, rational decisions or reasoned judgments affecting social, economic, legislative, and political issues?
7. What conditions are needed to compel a hypnotic subject to do something "against their will?"
8. Discuss the mechanism of this process in terms of the Trance Model, with examples.
9. Pick any religious or spiritual or New Age guru and explicitly describe their techniques. Identify trance generating loops, which cognitive functions that are disabled, and calculate the wyrd. Note if trances are terminated or if complex trances are created. Can you explicitly expose and describe the taboo of a specific religious trance technique or situation?
10. Find examples of the use of fear to disable critical judgment. Discuss the ways critical judgment can be re-enabled at any point during the production of fear.

Addiction

Here's One For The Road!

Are all addictions a kind of trance? Certainly trance narrows attention and can evoke compulsive, repetitive behaviors, just like an addiction. Addictions also share some of the same disabled cognitive functions you find in meditation and hypnotic trances such as short term memory loss, faulty or disabled critical thinking, mistaken beliefs and delusions, compulsive dwelling on the past, etc. Superficially then, common addictions share many characteristics with trance.

Although most addictions are destructive, some addictions—such as the addiction that an artist may have for his art—have creative characteristics. Love attachments can also be described as addictive; perhaps appropriately when relationships are destructive, but the longevity of old love relationships often provoke respect rather than pity. Also, some religious persons may be so devoted towards God that they lose contact with the ordinary world; we hardly term this kind of devotion an addiction. Rather, many people admire this sort of an addiction, especially when a religious addict is compulsively compassionate or devoted to helping the poor and sick. Yet, in some sense even such compulsive religious devotions can become as destructive as a drug addiction.

While I have named a specific type of trance structure "addictive," I also wanted to note that not all trances of this type are destructive. I also considered naming this type of trance structure "divine," but that had too many religious connotations. Besides, we live in a world where addiction is so common, it might be more useful to stay with the "addictive" term for this type of trance, but at the same time realize that addiction is not always negative. It can also be creative, socially useful, and have very positive effects on others. The difference is whether or not we have control over the trance. Most people cannot control their addictive trances, and this seems to be the main objection to addictions.

As you will discover, gaining control over an addictive trance is not easy, but once you understand the addictive trance structure, it becomes possible to change or terminate ordinary addictions. Then you have a powerful mental tool at your disposal.

Definition of an Addictive Trance

Addictive trances are composed of three trances: a meditation type of trance and two hypnotic types. These three trances work off each other and form a kind of lock, but each has a distinct trance generating loop and distinct sets of disabled cognitive functions. Generally, and first of all, a meditation trance creates a trance with disabled critical judgment and short term memory loss; these together create a taboo[37]—which is to say, the loop becomes secret even to yourself. Specifically, there is a mental loop of some sort; the content may just be words, or it may be feelings.

Subsequent to and within this meditation trance, a second trance is created: a hypnotic trance. Elements of the addiction are part of the second trance generating loop.[38] That is, within this second trance you will find such loop content as alcohol, drugs, behaviors, and so on, which usually identify or mark the addiction. This second trance is not usually a taboo but may be hidden or denied.

There is a third trance loop that connects the result of the second trance with the first. For example, when an alcoholic drinks himself or herself drunk, the physical result of drunkenness often results in guilt feelings. The suppression of these guilt

---

[37] The taboo in this case prevents access to the trance loop.
[38] A deep hypnotic trance will also be an addictive trance.

feelings are usually part of the process of the first meditation trance. The third loop needs to be repeated many times before a trance is created. However, it is the third loop that locks in the addiction and makes it compulsive and out of control.

While this definition is for the simplest form of an addictive trance, practically, there are usually more than one addictive trances in persons who have an addiction.[39] So, addictions tend to present themselves as complex forms of multiple trances. When multiple loops are involved, the combined trance wyrd also becomes strong. The memory loss effects of multiple trances really does block out the first meditation loop; in doing so, this strong taboo strengthens the trance wyrd.

One effect of the addictive trance structure produces a slowly repeating pain-pleasure cycle. A characteristic of the addictive structure is that interrupting any of the hypnotic trance loops is not effective in permanently breaking the addictive trance; the deeper meditation trance loop working its taboo magic continues to re-establish the hypnotic trances. Whenever an old trigger in the hypnotic trance loop is fired, an hypnotic trance can be reestablished. The effect is that an alcoholic compulsively, automatically, and often unconsciously, takes the first drink that re-establishes the pattern.

Thus, in alcohol addictions those who wish to break their addiction should not take the first drink. It is this first drink that is the old trigger in one of the hypnotic trance loops. It can be easily seen that substituting a religious behavior for a drink does not terminate the addictive trance structure; it merely modifies the addiction to an arguably more benign form. A more permanent approach would be to discover the first meditation trance loop and expose and de-construct the taboo. This will weaken the wyrd and can result in the collapse of the entire addictive trance.

I make an assumption about what is desirable in life, and I should state it explicitly. I assume that a robust life is a life of variety and wide options and that an impoverished life is a life with few options and little variety. Life naturally contains limits

---

[39] Alcoholics might smoke or have behavioral compulsions.

and limits help to restrain chaos and thus to free a certain kind of energy. Although there are many people of the opinion that all limits are bad, I feel that limits alone are not bad, in fact, limits are necessary to empower creativity. However, certain types of strict limits in life seem to imply the presence of a pathological state or at least delusions about lack of personal power. There is a delicate balance between the limits that empower personal growth and the limits that crush human spirit.

One way to find this balance is to realize that within any personal psychological reality there is a set of changing stimuli and response potentials. A behavior is a specific stimulus with its response, and a behavior results in a new stimulus, which joins other stimuli in creating the personal psychological reality. Theoretically, the responses that may exist for a given set of stimuli can be counted. The number of such potential responses is often thought of as the "richness" of a person's life. A relatively low number of potential responses or options indicates a relatively impoverished reality.

A healthy, normal psychological life seems to be one in which there is a rich set of stimuli and a rich set of responses. Furthermore, the pattern of behavior tends not to be rigidly repetitive and this rich variety seems to allow both personal growth and to stimulate others in their own search for variety and richness in life. On the other hand, an addictive personality could be characterized as one in which there are few responses and the pattern of behavior is generally repetitive.

What I find to be interesting is to apply the principles of trance theory to a wide variety of individual and institutional behaviors that appear to be rigid or repetitive—that is, presumable trances—and try to determine what the trance generating loops are, what the characteristics of the dissociated trance planes are, and how one might describe any created trance wyrds.

Any person has the potential to be in a trance as soon as their attention is limited. Ordinary concentration, when the mind is focused on a specific problem or thought, sets one of the conditions for a normal trance to occur. Intense pleasure, when the mind is engaged in joyful or exciting repetitive activity, sets an important condition for trance and may, for many people, become a trance. When one is daydreaming, with no specific direction of the thoughts, yet with a certain repetition of feelings, one is in a normal daydreaming trance. The general characteristic of these normal trance states seems to be that thoughts repeat and there is a limiting of attention; however, they can be easily interrupted. What makes a normal trance normal is primarily that it is easily interrupted. That is, specifically, disturbing the trance generating loop makes the dissociated trance plane collapse. Depending on many factors, such as the presence of secondary trance generating loops, or if the dissociated trance plane is so stable that disturbing the trance generating loop only makes more or different dissociated trance planes—hallucinations—such trances would appear less normal and more weird. For example, if you attempt to have a conversation with an alcoholic, you may succeed in interrupting one dissociated trance plane only to find that another dissociated trance plane has come into existence. This is one of the weird but expected results one obtains when conversing with alcoholic trance addicts. Some of them we can term pathological, and we can describe them in terms of trance theory.

In order to make wise decisions, it is necessary to have a wider state of awareness and consciousness and not a narrow one. It is necessary to have an overview of the long-range consequences of your decisions and not a narrow view, which comes from the immediate satisfaction of personal desire. With so many desirable objects in the world, and so much new information, how do you increase your awareness and wisdom?

Many kinds of consciousness raising activities try to promote the possibility that there are other ways to see or to understand life. In a larger field of awareness of possibilities, a more mature and integrated awareness can develop, resulting in less fear of chaos as well as a more open potential of being.

Psychologists and psychiatrists try to widen the perceptions of their clients, to promote new ways of handling stress and uncomfortable feelings without escape or denial. It is these wider perceptions, with more robust psychological options of action in life that enriches life, and not necessarily more material possessions in life.

Psychically, the narrowing of perception and the limiting of options or making an object of the sources of personal happiness, personal salvation, and personal betterment gives rise to ideas such as heaven, God, a Savior, a cult of personality, brand loyalty, and patriotism. Generally, the narrowing of perception produces hypnotic trance. In severe or pathological cases, the narrowing of perception produces paranoia, schizophrenia, violence, and addictions of all sorts.

Making an object out of our perceived source of happiness, salvation, and betterment also promotes the idea that there are "good," "moral," or "ethical" things and behaviors. That is, there is the perception that some "things" are better than other "things." And therefore, some things are worse, or even "sinful." It is often believed by some people that dope is bad, guns are bad, and money is "the root of all evil." These beliefs about dope, guns, and money come naturally from the idea that "things could be better, and the world would be a whole lot better if (dope, guns, or money) didn't exist." There is really no justification for empowering an object or a thing with the qualities of good or evil, except in the case of a narrowed perception and hallucinated projections. But it is precisely this narrowed perception or the hallucinated projections from the dissociated trance plane on to the object that causes dysfunction to arise in the psyche, in the individual, and in all social institutions and in the environment itself.

Learning something new utilizes dissociation as abstraction, but employing the hallucinated projections from the dissociated trance plane is not learning.

Sometimes it is argued that calling a thing "good" is merely a shorthand way of saying something more complex and a shorthand way of providing a sort of synopsis, saving time and avoiding a detailed description. The "good/bad" judgment is merely a way that an experienced authority can communicate the bottom line to someone, without needing to go through a tedious list of conditions and assumptions that underlie the ultimate judgment. Of course, the experienced authority can have false experience or have a hidden agenda that makes any judgments coming from such an authority immediately suspicious. Furthermore, the conditions may be falsely enumerated, and the logic supporting the "good" judgment may also be faulty. Usually, people find themselves arguing the "goodness" of a thing on precisely these terms: that one has faulty assumptions or faulty logic, or one has a hidden agenda that biases perception. Someone may ultimately admit that they only have a "belief" that the thing is "good," or that their judgment is merely a personal opinion, which cannot be supported by the facts. When there are multiple hallucinated projections on to objects, people, and situations, one belief will compete with all other beliefs, arguments will abound between one group with the Holy Writ against another group that is divinely inspired. It is quite simply lunatics arguing among delusions.

The self-searching individuals naturally wish to escape this madness. Some will evolve to new forms. Many will escape by dropping out. Dropping out often takes an addictive form. Alcohol, drugs, religion, work, over consumption, and TV are only a few of the more obvious forms of addictions. In many cases the dropping out takes the form of a desire to be in a trance that is induced or supported by substances like alcohol and drugs, or by social forms such as religion, work, consumption, or by more individual forms such as TV, love, overeating, violence, etc.

We share trances for the effects of trance, that is, for the effects brought about by an altered cognition space.

With less awareness of pain whether it is emotional, physical, or ontological and with less awareness of the wide variety of choices that exist in an enabled and robust reality, the person in a trance happily chooses among an impoverished and smaller set of options.

Life, perhaps, would be too difficult if people were always aware of their bodies, always had a perfect memory, always made perfect judgments, and were always aware of the infinite possibilities of life. Because most people cannot stand pain, because most people fear chaos, uncertainty, and death, most people enter into social, institutional, and mutual personal trances in order to reduce awareness. Perhaps, in the not too distant past, life was uncertain—in times of war or in hunger, poverty, fear, and abuse situations—and it made sense to hide and to create trance by singing ourselves songs, or saying prayers, or by putting our minds on certain constant images or visions. This is indeed how natural trances are created; the usual reason is to hide from something.

By a mutual trance, I mean that each of us in various ways and by social behavior supports an impoverished awareness in others. Our purposes in supporting impoverished awareness are: to be able to have some peace ourselves and to reduce the noise and the pain. Again, the reason for this is to reduce our awareness of the reality of chaos and escape the pain of the human condition. There is also some pleasure in entering trance in spite of the fact that trance reduces awareness.

If we speak of degrees of trance, it is my opinion that there is only a difference in degree between passively watching TV, ordinary rational thought, rigorous scientific thought, religious fervor, addictive states, and the states of mind belonging to mass murderers. All of the mind states above represent differing degrees of trance states.

There is also a strong similarity between addictions, hypnotic trance, and "altered states of consciousness." All of these "non-normal" states come about first by the progressive narrowing of perception and the limiting of awareness to a single or at most very few objects of attention. The narrowing of attention can be induced by drugs, chanting, television, etc. Second, an association must be made that connects every attempt to make the attention wider to an effort to make the attention more narrow. This association will serve to concentrate attention on the objects of attention. Third, when the association is strong enough, the original impulse to narrow attention can be removed. The reason is that the strong association already created will continue the attention toward the few objects.

Tribes, cults, societies, and nations inculcate restricted social behaviors through trance, training, customs, and laws because it requires simply too much cognitive processing overhead to understand the new or unusual behaviors of people. In primitive and ignorant societies new and unusual people are simply killed. In some ways the presence of trance inductive mechanisms—such as TV—helps to limit the awareness of the ignorant and therefore the more unusual people have more of a chance to survive if they don't watch TV themselves. This in itself is probably a positive evolutionary phenomenon.

It may seem bizarre to advocate the development of more intense trances and limited awareness and more impoverished realities as a global solution to social ills, yet with drug addiction, religions, and television isn't that precisely what seems to be happening? Let's understand what it is we are really doing and do it more efficiently! In America, according to the A.C. Nielsen Co. more than ninety-nine percent of the homes have a television, and the daily average time spent in front of a television is in excess of four hours, people may believe themselves to be informed, but their realities are severely impoverished.

When people walk around with their virtual reality helmets, trance music reverberating in the vacuum of inner space, they may believe themselves to be "connected" to the Host and King of the information mountain, but they will be only aware of a certain limited class of toxic atmospheric discharges and social inequities. They will be unaware of the fact of their own abuse.

In lieu of a fearless awareness of an enriched life, most people have chosen the way of impoverished and addictive trances. Let it be. Tranceless awareness is not for everyone. There are many examples of pathological trance. Identifying them as examples of the application of trance theory may be a step in the direction for positive change.

When the individual suffers, the family suffers. Dysfunctional, dropped-out, individuals in addictive trances place tremendous pressures on their families. As individuals experiencing the results of family members going through addictive behaviors are themselves stressed, it is no wonder that families disintegrate. When families don't disintegrate, there are often the side effects of child and spouse abuse or more serious social crimes. Disintegrated families result in homeless or nomadic gangs. Nomadic gangs are common in cities and are symptomatic of the underlying dysfunction. Cities become more difficult to manage when family and individual dysfunction becomes widespread and affects social institutions. After all, the social institutions can only reflect the individuals who run them.

Former Governor Lamb of Colorado has identified the dysfunctional institution in his own state and recognizes the same institutional dysfunctions on all levels of government. Widespread individual and institutional dysfunction destroys social assets. Dysfunction destroys people, jobs, the connectivity of the social fabric, and the pertinence of institutions. Institutions cease to be efficient and themselves become dysfunctional. While social resources and government assets can support dysfunctional institutions in times of chaos, in extreme cases and over the long term these resources and assets eventually are depleted, worn out, used up, and become useless or self-destructive. This characteristic of extremely dysfunctional institutions is more common in third-world countries.

Social dysfunctions can all be traced back to the pernicious effects of hypnotic and addictive trance at the individual level.

A habit usually is a long and complex trance generating loop and therefore when done only a few times represents a weak trance, that is, a trance with an unstable dissociated trance plane. Yet, when the habit is done hundreds or thousands of times, the behavior may become compulsive and appear like an addiction. In such a case, there is a more stable trance wyrd with constructive trance generating loops.

Socially or economically reinforced habits such as shaking hands, smoking cigarettes, having sex in the missionary position, wearing clothes when in society, answering the telephone when it rings, flushing the toilet after it is used, coming home after work and turning the TV on, all represent habits that are socially or economically supported in most countries of this world. Often the individual effort needed to break such trances is more than is possible to do. Such social habits or trances represent deep trances with trance wyrd components and secondary order constructive trance generating loops.

Breaking such trances increases the awareness of individual chaos, uncertainty, and pain. The sense of chaos, or fear, uncertainty, and pain is the reaction that is caused by attempting to change or modify the trance wyrd.

One could characterize this situation as an entrancement by magic.

One must be quite courageous to attempt to modify a trance wyrd. In addition, the trance analysis needed to break a trance is often a complicated and difficult undertaking. There is also no guarantee that even if the underlying trance generating loops were known, it would be possible to break the trance easily.

Love is a human emotion created socially often through a period of courtship and intimacy, desire, fantasy, physical contact, and orgasm.

The courtship, when it exists, often or typically occurs during primary trance inductive social situation such as dancing, listening to music, etc. These primary inductive social trance situations may produce many of the disabled cognitive conditions characteristic of trance, including faulty or failed memory, hallucinations, fixed attention, lack of volition, inability to make judgments, increased self-observation, dissociation, etc.

Love also has secondary inductive characteristics, insofar as courting individuals often speak of family, feelings, etc. These subjects often contain triggers to prior trance states. For example, when two people speak of personal experiences within their own family experiences, they may use words that trigger prior trance states. Dating and touching also may trigger somatic trances. Intimate touching will trigger prior somatic trance states including dissociation, lack of volition, fixed attention, etc.

When intimacy is coupled with physical release or relaxation such as orgasm, there is established a secondary order trance generating loop to enable these trance states.

The trance generating loop of love is characteristic of an addictive or hypnotic trance in the sense that the pathway of the secondary trance generating loop contains some external or physical component, and the dissociated trance plane leads back to the physical component.

There are many types of love trances. Some love trances may also have high components of the trance wyrd, but usually there are secondary order trance generating loops present.

Addiction can be better understood if you think of it not merely as "substance abuse" or performance addiction, but as a form of an impoverished reality that is maintained by a trance. Limited awareness, tunnel vision, the special characteristic that identifies a dysfunctional, impoverished reality, also identifies a type of trance state that may be also a characteristic of all addictions.

While pathological trances are not at all desirable, most people nearly all of the time are either in a pathological trance or are engaged in trying to get others into trance. It is precisely pathological trance, not the yogic trance, that permeates most of our waking social reality. It seems to me that once we can identify these pathological trances on a personal and social level, we can take steps to avoid them.

Perhaps the most important aspect of pathological trance is that it creates an unawareness or a "sleeping state." When your thoughts are limited in variety and your attention becomes fixed, the fixation alters perceptions; it can create dream states, visions, and hallucinations. In this sleeping state you are unaware of new information. Entranced by the street magician, you are unaware that the pickpocket has removed your wallet. The pathological trance state can create illusions that do not exist and cause the failure to perceive what does exist. Not all trances are pathological; the trance state of a yogi can be a tool to illuminate what is not normally perceived.

According to the Substance Abuse and Mental Health Services Administration it is estimated that over twenty-two million individuals have a substance dependence or abuse problem in the US. Such addictions include drug and alcohol addictions (now termed "substance abuse" to include cocaine, psychedelics, caffeine, nicotine, as well as alcohol, sugar, chocolate, and junk-food), TV addiction, work-related addictions, sex and love addictions, food related addictions, computer addictions, and other behavioral or performance addictions. Addictions commonly share the characteristic that a socially dysfunctional behavior is present and the addict has progressively fewer and fewer performance options resulting in an impoverished reality. High percentages of addiction are found not only in America. Russia has its problems with vodka. India and the Middle East have their opium addicts, and Switzerland and Japan have their work junkies. The personal life disruption and social costs are well-documented and the costs are probably well underestimated.

Alcohol addiction is a worldwide phenomenon. Even strict Islamic and Hindu cultures have their share of alcoholics. Alcohol is widely available in all industrial nations and cultures. Alcohol addiction is merely one way that addiction manifests, yet the social costs of alcohol addiction alone are immense.

Drug addiction is also a worldwide phenomenon. The drugs may vary depending on the culture, the law, and the severity of punishment. In the case of tobacco, it has been shown that nicotine is more addictive than heroin, and yet in many parts of the world the consumption of nicotine is not only tolerated, but actually encouraged. The long-term health effects of tobacco use, while widely known, are ignored. The use of drugs, whether nicotine, caffeine, heroin, cocaine, marijuana, designer drugs, or sugar has, like alcohol, immense long-term health and social costs.

Knowing that one addiction can be substituted for another fairly easily provides a clue to a therapeutic approach to addictions in general. For example, alcoholics can be induced to trade their alcohol addiction for a type of quasi-religious addiction. Alcoholics Anonymous (AA) programs also prove "successful" with sex and love addicts, overeaters, Synanon, etc. Some heroin addicts can be induced to swap their heroin for methadone treatment. Therapists know that addictions are often found together, for example cigarettes and alcohol, and that the person who is addicted to one substance or practice can be induced to either add other addictions or to swap them for others.

The fact that one addiction can be substituted for another fairly easily provides a clue to a therapeutic approach to addictions in general. Bandler and Grinder have shown that a process of pacing and leading can, over time, limit awareness and induce trance. With appropriate conditions, it is perhaps possible to pace and lead addictive personalities into a wider and richer reality. In this way, addicts can be "deprogrammed," without programming them into another addiction. The general goal is to program them into a rich reality where the object of a past addiction exists, but along side with a much larger set of attractive possibilities. When this occurs, it is impossible to distinguish a prior addict from a "normal" person by behavior alone. It certainly is not desirable to negatively reinforce addictive syndromes. To do so runs the risk of modeling "drug switching," which is not a true cure.

It is often thought that addictions come about due to the stresses of modern life, through childhood experiences, through trauma, disability, or genetic predisposition. No one seems to know for certain. Perhaps because addictions are so prevalent, it impossible to know what a non-addictive state is like.

A great deal of inconsistent social, religious, personal, economic, and political energy is spent in attempting to rid the world of addictive substances. Except for societies that employ ruthless and absolutist methods, the energy spent in riding the world of these "sinful substances" does seem neither very successful nor cost-effective. Arguments have been made that the anti-"sinful substance" zealots may themselves be dysfunctional in addictive and pathological ways.

Religious addictions seem harmless enough. A 1990 survey of 113,000 people around the United States by the Graduate School of the City University of New York found that ninety percent of Americans identify themselves as religious. Practicing Christians, Scientologists, Muslims, Jehovah's Witnesses, Masons, Buddhists, Hindus, Jews, and Mormons have no other bad habits than occasionally proselytizing, sometimes imposing their ideas on others. Since the religious generally have fewer other "bad" habits, and religion seems to promote a certain tribal social adhesion, religions are not usually thought of as being symptomatic of a problem, but rather, perhaps, as part of a solution. On the other hand, religious addiction often carries with it an intransigence and intolerance of other points of view that can prove as dangerous as a drug addict with a loaded gun. When religious fervor is combined with the rule of law and armed with deadly force, religious addicts effectively prevent the evolution of a better type of human being.

Religious cults often use methods that induce trance. Peer pressure, confessional types of testimonials, sense deprivation, lack of contradicting perspectives or viewpoints, hysteria, and hyper-emotionalism all act to constrain awareness and to increase suggestibility. Repetition continued over time will give rise to trance states, which with second order trance loops can certainly become addictive. Confession, for example, used as a catharsis, is a second order stress-relieving trance loop, which reinforces the belief trance state.

Addiction can be better understood if you think of it not merely as "substance abuse" or "performance addiction," but as a form of hypnotic trance that is maintained by a second order trance loop. Limited awareness and tunnel vision are the special characteristics that identify a dysfunctional, impoverished reality, and also identify those pathological trance states characteristic of all addictions.

Meditative trance states, which are similar to hypnotic trance states, can also be termed addictive if they are an end in themselves. Religious fervor, as a state which feeds upon itself without end, is also quite definitely an addiction as defined by the Trance Model. Certain political and power syndromes also may be termed addictive if they result in an impoverished reality.

The trance aspect of addiction deserves some comment. In extreme addictions there may be no other awareness except the desire for the addictive substance and how to get it. Presumably, it is because of the limited awareness on a "substance" that such substances have a bad name. It is not easy or convenient to blame a pattern or a process, since patterns and processes are so hard to identify, don't occupy space, don't have weight, and can't be taxed.

The trance-induction potential of television is well-known and is used commercially for manipulating consumer tastes as well as other ideas. However useful television is for commercial and control reasons, it cannot be reasonably argued that promoting an impoverished reality is, in the end, really socially beneficial. Or can it?

The addiction to TV, for example, comes about first by having a mild interest in a specific TV program, narrowing of perception to the TV screen, listening to the voices and music, and watching the scenes as they develop. Second, pleasurable associations through the use of triggers within the program should stimulate fantasies, hallucinations, and dreams as a means of escape from everyday responsibilities or stress. In general, if a viewer likes a specific program, this association is easily made. TV producers spend a lot of effort to make TV productions pleasurable and escapist. Third, when there is no more stress and no more everyday responsibilities, the pleasure that can be derived from watching TV must be high enough so that it is immaterial whether the use of TV is specific to stress removal or not. The addiction to TV will then be established.

The person who is able to put long, continuous hours into a difficult job may be capable to doing this only if in a trance. The pleasures of an engaging job can produce feelings of timelessness. Repetitive jobs narrow the attention to only the work at hand. Part of the mind is engaged in the job, but another part of the mind is free to dream. The dream-state produced is exactly characteristic of trance. In this dream-state, the work is being performed, but the worker is not necessarily aware of working. He may be visualizing a beach, having sexual or power fantasies, or other hypnoidal and hypnotic dreams. The worker seems aware, but is really in a trance with reduced awareness.

Work addicts are almost revered for their devotion to their work. Calvin and Zwingli have convinced entire societies that the person who works and makes money is closer to God and has most assuredly has an eternal lease in one of heaven's plushier communities. Employers love work addicts, because this devotion enhances profit. Work addictions are not limited to any one particular industry. As a professional computer consultant, I have seen how some employers shamelessly exploit willing computer programmers who are addicted to computers.

Trance in the work place makes it easier to control information and employees. If an employee only does the job in front of his nose and knows neither what others are doing nor how they do it, that employee will never become a threat to the owners of the business nor raise embarrassing social or political questions. One presumes—falsely—that the owners of a business would be the only ones who would be aware of what their business is really doing. Yet, owners are themselves often in a trance and many times keep their attention only on the "bottom line." They, too, may be unaware of the social or environmental impacts of their business. Unfortunately, one of the disastrous side effects of most trances is that they not only inhibit awareness, but they also disable communication. One cannot communicate what one is unaware of.

Work related addictions first require that the perception is narrowed to work or to work-related things and activities. Second, non-work related activity should be perceived as a source of stress, something to be avoided. The rewards of work should be limited to the perfection of the work itself, so that work is the means to the end. Finally, when work-pleasure or perfection-pleasure is self-sustaining, the reason for work can be progressively reduced or removed. The stress produced will serve to drive the worker harder into his work, rather than to reduce his production or concentration on work.

One of the most serious social side-effects of pathological work trances is the resulting reduced awareness and disabled communication. Communication of information is critical for any system to function. Human systems as well as computer systems, and other ecological, biological, political, and social systems, require clear, accurate, timely communication of information in order to function properly. The lack of clear, accurate, or timely communication between individuals may be the basis for misunderstandings, disappointments, hurt feelings, resentment, and violence. The economic, agricultural, industrial, and social systems that rely on people who are in pathological trances can have and often have disastrous breakdowns.

Pathological trances are, unfortunately, almost universally encouraged within businesses, the military, and governmental organizations. The more an employee can, with single-minded determination, execute the orders and policies of his organization, the more that employee is rewarded, promoted, and respected. Single-mindedness, however, is indicative of trance and possibly a pathological trance. And the existence of a trance always implies that there are areas where the employee remains unaware. Therefore, the single-mindedness that is rewarded in many large institutions actually contributes to long-term organizational dysfunction.

Where organizations advertently or inadvertently encourage trance in their employees, since trance disables communication, one should not be surprised when there are system dysfunctions whether in business, the military, or in government.

When, unlike a yogi, we do not choose our trances and we are unaware of the types and nature of the pathological trances in our lives, then there are things of which we are unaware. What we are unaware of causes more human suffering than the sometimes painful knowledge of the truth. One goal of a robust life is to be as aware as possible of our real options. When our unconscious pathological trances cripple our options, the result is often disaster and tragedy in our personal lives, our society, and for the environment.

Related to work addiction is a phenomenon more akin to what people often appreciate as "artistic inspiration" or artistic drive. An artist may spend long hours with a project that consumes his energy, perhaps stresses his family, and finally results in a creation. What distinguishes this artistic drive from addiction is that the artistic drive is not a closed loop. That is, eventually the behavior comes to an end. However, if the behavior does not terminate, but is repetitive with increasingly limited responsiveness to the outside world, therapists term the behavior dysfunctional and perhaps even "addictive." If the behavior has no end other than a "life style," for example, a therapist can readily identify the behavior as an addiction of a sort that does not end.

A goal of therapy is personal empowerment, the discovery and ending of unconscious compulsions, and the enrichment of choice. My perspective is that such therapy is equivalent to becoming aware of our trances and knowing how to control or terminate them. It is not merely interesting to consider the type of society that might emerge when we control our trances, it may well determine our survival as individuals as well as the planet.

If you really want to get into a pathological trance and stay there, here's a general recipe. First, you must impoverish your reality by removing all distractions and limiting your awareness to a single or at most a very few objects of attention. This narrowing of attention can be helped along by the passions inspired by drugs or trauma, by joining some religious or political movements, or by staying at home and watching a lot of television or engaging your computer. It would be a good idea to get rid of distractions like kids, magazines, or books—especially books that give you options or make you think about other possibilities. Secondly, you must convince yourself that all other options—outside of your chosen perfect ideal, of course—are "evil" and that every attempt that your "monkey mind" makes to have variety must be crushed and that you must keep your mind "pure" and only allow thoughts about your chosen passion. This mental trick will serve to concentrate your attention firmly on the object of your monomania. A second order loop that reinforces or rewards your monomania in such a regular and consistent way that even pain does not deter you will "fix" your trance. You will then be entranced in a pathological trance.

While pathological trances are not at all desirable, most people, most of the time, are either in a trance or are engaged in trying to get others into one. It is precisely pathological trance, not the yogic trance, that permeates most of our waking reality. It seems to me that once we can identify these pathological trances on a personal level, we can take steps to avoid them.

If trance is defined as fixated thinking, then nearly all human activities create some type of trance. The bounded circles of thinking that keep us in trances are countless. The entire "ordered universe" is a trance. But there is an escapist's pleasure in remaining in trance and a deep human fear of the chaos that can result if there were no trance to "order" to life.

Terminating Addictive Trances

Start at any place in your addictive trance. Addictive trances reward an impoverished thought-set. You can help reduce any addiction by rewarding the enrichment of your thoughts. This means expanding the variety of your thoughts without trying to remove the thoughts you think are the problem. Continue expanding and enriching your thoughts through new and stimulating ideas, people, and experiences. When the variety of your thoughts becomes robust, ideas will be self-generating and the addictive trance will naturally cease to exist, by definition.

One effective way is to find the trance generating loop and replace one element in that loop. Wait until the dissociated trance plane changes, then replace a second element. Continue until the second order dissociated trance plane is unstable enough so that you can attack the primary trance generating loop. Once you destroy the primary trance generating loop, the addictive trance will stop.

Limited awareness, the special characteristic that defines a dysfunctional, impoverished reality, also defines a type of trance state that may be characteristic of a posthypnotic state. Certainly those who have delusions can be considered to be in a trance of some sort. But of what sort is it?

Compulsive repetition; memory defects leading to various types of amnesia, faulty registration and recall; and reactive confabulations and misidentifications resulting in disorientation can suggest either schizophrenic psychosis, a wide variety of organic brain disorders, or a pathological trance.

Even a neurotic's inability to abandon old and disadvantageous patterns of reacting suggests that a repetitive and compulsive behavior is due to some type of pathological trance. That is, it may not be enough to point out or interpret unconscious mental contents without simultaneously investigating the possible existence of primary and secondary trance generating loops, and examining the nature of the dissociated trance planes as well as of the trance wyrds that are created by such loops.

It is known that simple and uncomplicated repetitive behavior can be terminated through vigorous stimulation, except when there is a gross defect in attention. Trance too can be terminated, except when the dissociated trance plane contains secondary loops or when multiple dissociated trance planes exist whose combined trance wyrd components exceed the energy available to the normal ego structure. In such cases trance termination is very difficult.

Since, normally, trance reduces body awareness, memory functions, judgment, etc., it is undesirable to indefinitely prolong trance or to create habitual trance states. To do so increases the potential that the body or ego structure becomes damaged and that subsequent action does not correspond to reality, becomes delusional. Although temporary trance states are in fact essential to an intelligent adaptation to life, prolonged trances produce a variety of effects, some of which can be termed pathological, but others of which can be termed remarkable and extraordinary.

Exercises

1. Identify one of your addictions. There are at least two loops in your addiction. One is inside your head; the other is partly outside your head. Describe, in writing, step by step, each element of both loops.
2. The internet is a big addiction for most people. Describe the loops that make up the internet trance. Estimate the wyrd for each loop and justify why you think the internet is such a big addiction.

Questions

1. Identify one pathological trance in your life.
2. The police often rigidly enforce traffic laws. Since this is a repeated loop in some sense, what is the nature of the dissociated trance that is produced in the police officer? What cognitive functions are disabled?
3. In some religious festivals self-flagellation occurs. This may be considered a trance generating loop. What is the nature of the trance that is produced? Is it an addictive, hypnotic, or meditation trance and why?

4. If a political policy is held in place by an addictive trance, what would be the venue of change according to the model?
5. Explain brand recognition in terms of addictive trance. What are the trance generating loops?

Charisma

Sweeping You Up into a Trance

There is a fourth type of trance that has a complex but interesting structure. It takes some time to create a charismatic trance and can be dangerous to do so, but a charismatic trance produces extremely strong wyrds. The charismatic trance wyrd is often so strong that you can even feel it at a distance and through walls. Certainly, when you are in the presence of someone who is adept at generating and maintaining a charismatic trance, you are compelled to go into a trance yourself; you really don't have any choice.

A charismatic trance is created primarily by a hypnotic trance loop, which is subsequently enhanced by a strong, secondary, internal trance generating loop. This is followed by a third hypnotic trance loop and finished when a fourth loop ties the third addictive trance to one of the other loops. The wyrd is strongest when a taboo covers and hides one or more of the primary loops.

A person who is generating this form of trance has one or more addictive trances present. At least one of the loops of the addictive trance involves other people, so it is also hypnotic. The effect of this addictive-hypnotic loop pulls people into a trance. If you pay any attention to the person who is generating this form of trance, even to understand them for a moment, you become caught up in a fascinating and addictive process, much the way a co-dependent gets involved with an alcoholic. Except it is much stronger, and more compelling. Naturally, you would expect that a person who generates a charismatic trance would be somewhat unusual. Occasionally, long-time alcoholics can demonstrate charismatic trance effects. Dry alcoholics, especially those who are also sociopaths, can exhibit this kind of trance as well. Psychosis may be seen as a presenting symptom of this type of trance. In general, a loop in the dissociated plane means a type of self-induced hypnosis is being created in which the ego predominates. It is a trance full of illusions, delusions, and hallucinations. Body awareness is minimal and so may be compassion. Most people in a charismatic trance do not have much compassion, because they are not concerned with the external as much as with serving their internal trance loops. Generally, those in a charismatic trance only feel the effects of their inner trance as real; they cannot feel others in an authentic way. In addition, their deepest primary loops are usually taboo, that is, secret or forgotten, or of such a frightening aspect that they are avoided at the conscious level. Examples of individuals in a charismatic trance include Svengali, Rasputin, Hitler, Jesus, the Buddha, and many other historically important social, political, and religious persons.

The nature of a charismatic trance implies that strong trance wyrds are created simply because of the additive effect formed by multiple trance loops. Although it may be tempting to try to create strong trance wyrds, I do not suggest that everyone should run out and try to generate a charismatic trance—on the contrary—the progressive training of the mind may enable some individuals to create strong charismatic trances that can be terminated at will. This will enable a person to be at choice. Nonetheless, this path is fraught with dangers.

I will discuss the charismatic trance from a technical as well as a practical point of view. My objective is for you to recognize, analyze, and know what is involved to learn how to control a charismatic trance. There are also three main perspectives: one perspective is from the point of the person who is generating the charismatic trance. Another perspective is from the point of the person who is affected by the charismatic trance. There is a third perspective I pursue is to not be the generator of a charismatic trance nor become swept up into them.[40]

Ego-maniacs, driven individuals on a "mission," certain kinds of visionaries, artists, or self-proclaimed messiahs, etc., are likely to be in charismatic trances in which the trance wyrds are so intense that they sweep up others into their trance by potentiating dissociated trance planes and constructing trance generating loops, often over a distance. Successful movie stars, gurus, saints, business and political leaders, and so forth, are all in charismatic trances.

The identifying characteristic of a charismatic trance is the existence of two hypnotic trance loops. The first loop contains a belief that they are on a mission; it has a fixed idea or focus. They compulsively talk about their "mission," and demonstrate ego-mania. The trance generating loop consists of the subject or focus of their mission. That is all that exists in their mind. Everything is about their "mission" or mania. If this first loop existed alone, by itself, they would seem to babble about their mania in a compulsive way, but you—the observer—would not be pulled into their babble. However, the second hypnotic loop goes from the outside to the inside; that is, they pull others into focusing energy on their mission. In other words, every idea other than the mania, is actively associated to the mania. It is this second loop that invites your participation, demands your focus, and, when repeated, draws you into a hypnotic trance. These two loops are distinct and separate. There may be other loops, as well, which help to fixate the two trances in place, but these two loops constitute the primary trances.

Because the resulting charismatic trance wyrds are strong, people will get swept up into them. Personality cults can result when people give up their own power to the person who is in a charismatic trance. Personal charisma resulting in political power can be a result of a well-managed charismatic trance.

---

[40] But because many people *are* swept up into one or another charismatic trance, the third perspective may be seen as criticism of those who are involved in charismatic trance. I am not criticizing, *per se,* rather I am only trying to describe and understand what is going on with this most fascinating form of trance.

Entertainment figures who manage to create a charismatic trance can become famous.

Visionaries and prophets may also be in a charismatic trance and they can carry a positive evolutionary message. But the mere presence of a charismatic trance does not itself prove that any given charismatic person will use the trance in a positive way. The only thing that you can really say about a charismatic trance is "Wow, it sure is powerfully impressive." What people identify as "charisma" is just the effect of the trance wyrd.

The Structure

A charismatic trance starts with a meditation trance loop maintained over a long period of time. Opportunities for a long term submersion in a meditation trance are rare but do exist. For example, spending time in a monastery provides an opportunity for long term meditation. Another opportunity would be spending many years in prison, especially in solitary confinement. Yet another opportunity for developing a long term meditation trance is extreme pain or suffering, which may be the result of family abuse, a war, an injury, or an illness. The specific experience of pain is often the source of a specific taboo of which the meditation trance is the covering. This first building block of a charismatic trance—the pain, the meditation, and the taboo—requires time to fully develop. Chronic pain is another powerful stimulus to repeating something mentally in order to create pain relief and thereby create a trance generating loop. Denial too helps to develop the taboo and adds more wyrd to the charismatic trance. But this meditation trance is only the first part of the building block. I will refer to it later on.

A monk might use a mantra or prayer as the main meditation trance loop, but in order for a strong charismatic trance to develop, it is vital that the loop content not change much over time. There may be a tendency to augment or change the trance loop content due to the effect of the trance. For example, a monk might start off using a simple prayer, but over a period of time, might think that he has grown out of it and wish to change the prayer. This only serves to lessen the trance wyrd and will not result in a strong charismatic trance developing. A more effective way is to start another prayer or mantra without terminating the first one. That is, one adds an additional meditation trance loop to the first. This approach will definitely increase the wyrd.

The meditation trance created in the context of a prison environment can have as its content cognitive objects an association with memories that contribute to reliving the experience or the feelings of frustration and anger. These feelings and the experience that produces them become the taboo of which the meditation trance is the cover.

The effect of these prison-related meditation loops creates heightened inner involvement, memory modification, and some body anesthesia and pain relief.

Once a long term meditation trance is well established, another trance may be started, which involves the externally perceived world. This trance is the second building block of a charismatic trance. It is a hypnotic trance, but may not necessarily include people, per se. So, someone in a prison might look at a spider on a wall and associate the movement of the spider with a particular change in the first meditation trance. For example, if the spider moves up the wall, then the meditation focus is rage and revenge; if the spider moves down the wall, then the meditation focus is peace and forgiveness. For a monk there may be other associations—with church bells, for example, or with the nightly visits of a mouse. Either way, the external world is always experienced from the point of view of the first meditation trance. Although the monk or prisoner may have started with a meditation trance, integrating the content of the external world into the meditation trance is a certain and natural way to create a hypnotic trance in addition to the meditation trance.

In order to be able to control the charismatic trance, it is important that the monk or prisoner develops or creates a trigger for starting or stopping the trance. For a monk or prisoner this may be the dinner bell, but for someone in a family abuse situation it may be the touch or the voice of a favorite aunt or grandmother or even a family pet that can terminate a trance through passive intervention. This trigger, either in reality or as a memory, brings an important ground control to a trance.

Although I have been discussing the simplest structure of a charismatic trance, this structure actually becomes much more complicated in real life. By that, I mean in any charismatic trance there is not simply one meditation trance loop or one hypnotic trance loop. There are multiple trance generating loops, and these result in multiple trances creating complex systems, which can become a challenge to analyze.

A clear method of controlling such complex trance systems becomes very important. Without any definite control a trance complex[41] can eventually become disconnected from this reality resulting in trancelings, delusions, and entities seeming to have an independent existence. The point to remember is that each trance results in its own set of disabled cognitive functions, especially short-term memory. So, the person in a complex trance has many memory failures. Some of these memory failures are covering important taboos, keys to controlling the trance.

Sustained over time, any uncontrolled trance complex creates another reality for the person in the trance. In the case of the spiders, you can imagine that the person creating and living in such a charismatic trance would develop many delusions. Over time, a range of new perceptions and delusions—perceived from trance—forms a new reality in which the movement of the spider and the delusion of the meditator become one: one in the sense that it is really not known whether it is the movement of the spider creating the inner feelings or the inner feelings creating the movement of the spider. It becomes vital that the spider cooperate with the meditator in order to maintain a certain coherence of reality. I mean, the meditator begins to have a vested interest in the movement of the spider; the spider must cooperate with

---

[41]A trance complex is a system of trance generating loops creating multiple meditation, hypnotic, addictive, and charismatic trances. Such complexes are very difficult to control or break and frequently seem to have an independent life.

the meditator. This need or compulsion, springing from the long term meditation and hypnotic and addictive processes, which have created their own realities, is the structural mechanism that sweeps others into a kind of codependency. If you are going to become the spider on a prisoner's wall, you had better behave like one or you will be psychically crushed. Several "crushed spiders" later the prisoner/meditator begins to create a compelling wyrd. Charismatic personalities—those in a charismatic trance—are not rare.

Likewise, the lonely, isolated, hermit monk may begin to perceive religious artifacts and symbols in new ways. The artifacts may speak to him or appear to reveal hidden messages or meanings. Over time, the new relationship with the religious artifacts, caused by his impressions with the new "hidden symbolic meanings" alters the monk's perceptions and reality. Cognitive functions such as sensual perceptions, critical judgment, or memory do not function in a normal way. Developed into a charismatic trance, the hermit monk may become a visionary, a prophet, a mystic with new messages for mankind.

There is a temptation to describe such isolated prisoners or hermit monks as being delusional or psychotic. It is only when the trance generating loops become so numerous and have repeated so many times over a long period of time that they begin to have the potential to compel others. But the underlying mechanism is a complex trance process. An uncontrolled charismatic trance will seem delusional, of course. But, a well-defined and controlled charismatic trance pulls everyone into hypnosis; the shared reality is constructed. You can see what is not there; what is there is not seen. What you experience may well be miraculous; if a group agrees that they all saw the boy climb up the rope and disappear, who can say otherwise? If the vibuti[42] and the Rolex watch are real enough, is that not proof of a miracle? You may think of other examples of a charismatic trance.

---

[42] Sacred ash materialized by Satya Sai Baba, for example.

The Disabled Cognitive Functions

I mentioned above that the inner meditation trance has some pain relieving function through a decrease in body awareness. In addition, there almost certainly are changed perceptions due to the long term effects of maintaining an alternate reality or two or even more. The disabled cognitive functions are of course attached to various trances, but they have synergistic effects as well. That is, if one trance causes memory dysfunction, another trance can heighten perception in such a way as to create false memories. Critical judgment is disabled by the action of one trance, but enhanced literalism can create a type of false and delusional "logical" thinking that seems to mimic the normal critical judgment we have come to know and love on this planet. Yes, those in a charismatic trance do seem like they are from another planet where they can converse with invisible sky beings, talk to birds, and where water runs uphill. When maintained for a long time, these alternate realities[43] become more or less permanent. There is a vested interest by the meditator in maintaining the alternate reality. The long-term meditator has plenty of time to increase perception and develop operative skills in this new reality or realities so that the so-called "normal" reality is reinterpreted to fit the alternate reality. The spider does follow the desires of the meditator and the normal laws of physics don't apply any more.

The Clash of Realities

When a person not in trance comes into range of such a meditator, there is an initial clash of realities. Observing the person in a strong charismatic trance can provoke fear, but also high respect. There is a feeling of electricity in the air, also of excitement, possibly dread. These sensations are effects of the wyrd. One feels a shift in reality, like going into another dimension, into a tunnel or into a waking dream. It takes an extremely self-aware person to maintain conscious observer status in such wyrd fields.

---

[43] Most psychiatrists would term these "alternate realities" by the word "delusion."

The Wyrd

The wyrd is the trance force. It measures the strength or depth of a trance and measures the difficulty of breaking the trance. The wyrd is additive in the sense that multiple, interlocking trances are tough, resilient, and automatically reforming. You just add up the wyrds of all the component trances and that represents the total wyrd of that trance complex. In the case of a charismatic trance, there is the primary inner meditation trance, which may have continued for many years. Add to that the hypnotic trance involving the spider on the wall. Add to that the additional trances built on the alternate reality in which the meditator controls the spider. All of these trances take place over a long period of time, so the wyrd becomes numerically large.

The loops constituting these trance components must be sustained for a long period of time in order for the wyrd to grow in intensity. When the loops become fixed or compulsive due to interlocking loops, the wyrd will become so strong as to become palpable. Depending on the content of the constituted loops, the wyrd may be attractive or repulsive. It may be very scary or spooky as well.

Some of the primary loops may be taboo and covered, so that these loops are not locatable or they may be secret. Even exposing the taboo does not necessarily mean the trance is broken, although the wyrd may become less and some of the external hypnotic loops will become unstable; fewer people will be caught in the charismatic web.

Charisma from the Pedestrian View

So, you pass by a building or tent from which strange sounds emerge. You are immediately curious because the sounds are so unusual, and you feel something weird is going on. You are curious and you want to enter the building or tent. This is the effect of the trance wyrd generated by whoever is in the building or tent. It pulls you in. It attracts you in a wyrd way.

The sounds may not make much sense initially. In fact, they might be confusing. Part of you may be bored, but another part follows it and in order to make sense of it, you have to suspend judgment. But when you do, you experience a kind of pleasure or curious happiness, completeness. You begin to understand things from a new perspective. Some parts might not make sense yet, but as you have already seen, you need to suspend judgment. Then you can experience something pleasurable as well as have a new understanding. You feel as though you are achieving something positive and personal. Eventually, you simply believe that you will reach some higher goal and understand everything. And when that happens, you are sure to have even more understanding and pleasure. Even if understanding is not your goal, you can simply relax and have faith in your leader who will bring you to the goal.

Coupled with this grabbing, sucking type of trance web is your experience of becoming open, involved in something important beyond yourself, but at the same time you need to suspend more and more of your own critical judgment and abdicate personal responsibility over your own life. You feel open, but you actually have become literal-minded, quite narrow, dogmatic, fixed, and closed in order to accept the new paradigms of the leader.

Suspending critical thinking, as well as refraining from expressing any critical thoughts aloud are characteristic of those who are involved with someone in a charismatic trance.

Taboo becomes important in charismatic trance. There are feelings of secrecy, power, specialness. Added to this is also an unspoken and unspeakable fear, perhaps spookiness. Somehow you feel afraid to break away from the leader or to challenge him. It is as though your new world of special pleasure and knowledge would collapse and you would become insane, lose your bearings in life, be alone.

A charismatic trance is very seductive. In fact, if you love the leader, you will have even more understanding. It is—in a sense—addictive love that is fundamental to charismatic trance. With a charismatic trance you might feel more love,

117

companionship, and connectedness than you have ever felt before. Although the love felt for religious leaders is undeniable, alcoholics also feel love for each other, and the fans of entertainment stars also feel love for them. So, the love has to do with the trance and not with who is being loved, or what the love is about, or what values are being represented by the charismatic relationship.

The seductive relationship of charisma and the love that followers have for their leaders can also express itself in actual sexual relationships no matter what the expressed values of the leader may be. Sexual love and these feelings are taboo, however. Repressed sexual love serves to strengthen the wyrd in these forms of trance. Thus, practically speaking, sexuality in some form is often likely to be present as an expression of love and power. The repression of sexuality merely speaks of the taboo, and its presence efficiently increases the wyrd. The exposure of the taboo will in all cases tend to destabilize the hypnotic loops, weaken the wyrd, and may result in the termination of the charismatic trance.

Taboo covers the source of life as chaos. The potential energy of chaos is very primitive, violent, potentially murderous, but also incredibly beautiful, full of energy and power. In this bifurcated sense, chaos both creates and destroys life. This aspect of the divine is Dionysian. It represents the destruction of the individual ego and is the primordial separation of the Unity into Creation. Or, to put in other terms, the beginning of trance creates the separation between the Self and the Other. The Other is the Chaos. We stay with the Self in order to preserve ourselves. At the same time, we cover the trance with a taboo, forget about it as much as possible, and trick ourselves into thinking our illusory individual self is the Big Ego.

After losing our divine nature because of this trick, we can spend lifetime energy attempting to recover it. Cults and their charismatic leaders in various forms of evolution appear from time to time in an attempt to bring us individually back to our original hidden divine nature. And so it goes.

Exercises

1. Set a time—like an hour—for exposure to a charismatic cult, entertainment, or religious group. Write down your feelings and sensations during the hour, and especially if your short term memory fails. After no longer than one hour, leave the group and note your feelings. Can you identify the hypnotic loops? Can you estimate the intensity of the wyrd? What made it difficult for you to leave the group after one hour exposure?

2. Locate a mental institution in your neighborhood. As you get close to the mental institution how close do you need to be before you can detect the wyrd? What is the nature of the energy? How do you feel or think? Does prolonged exposure to the wyrd affect your short-term memory or your critical judgment? How do you know?

3. Determine who in the mental institution has the strongest wyrd. Sometimes this can be done with a sociogram, but asking nurses or inmates can help identify the one with the strongest wyrd. Try to identify the individual loops which create the charismatic trance. Spend one hour (only) with that individual. Note especially the effect of the wyrd on your own subjective feelings and any hypnotic trances induced in you. Be aware especially of meditative trance loops started in you. Note the trance delta and trance epsilon.

Questions

1. Name any current political leader who you believe is in a charismatic trance. Describe the characteristics of the trance and how the political nature of the charismatic trance has helped or hurt the social order.

2. What are some of the ways any political charismatic trance could be mitigated?

Invasive Trance

A Step Forward is a Step Back

An invasive trance is an hypnotic trance created by a hypnotist who takes advantage of a condition of your mind, which sometimes occurs when you are more suggestible than normal.

An opportunity to create an invasive trance is created whenever your critical judgment is not enabled or you are not alert and not thinking critically. This can happen if you are drugged or drunk, but may also happen when you are simply not alert, not paying attention, distracted, confused, afraid, or over-stimulated. There are many opportunities for an invasive trance to be started whether you are in a busy city, a jungle, or living alone as a hermit.

Invasive trances are hypnotic and the loops contain suggestions that create or alter beliefs, change performance, or suggest that a future conditional specific action is to take place. Under normal circumstances, we might believe that there is no one interested in manipulating us, and this is the reason we are usually not in a state of alertness. Invasive hypnotic trance techniques work primarily because we are not aware that they could be working. Hypnotists who wish to use these techniques would prefer that we would not know about or be alert to their use. Invasive trance techniques are mind control techniques based on deception, secrecy, and stealth.

If we were always alert for mind-control over us, we would be considered to be paranoid. And yet, the technology has existed for invasive mind control for many decades. We might love to think that it has never been used on us personally, but this would be a mistake. The extent of the use of mind-control technology is not really known, but it has been used opportunistically in military theaters, as well as in commercial and religious enterprises.

The following are a few documented examples in which invasive trance techniques have been used:

During the first Gulf War, the United States used an unusual but effective means of forcing surrender of Iraqi troops. High above ground a specially equipped AWAC aircraft broadcast microwaves. These microwaves carried a non-sinusoidal[44] sub-carrier of approximately 15K Hertz—a frequency just above the audible range for humans. And on this sub-carrier was a frequency-modulated sub-carrier of audible frequencies with an Arabic voice delivering hypnotic suggestions designed to compel the Iraqi forces to surrender. The news at that time reported, without explanation, that thousands of Iraqi troops surrendered, sometimes waving a white flag to empty or abandoned US Military vehicles.[45]

A company in the United States has perfected a technique of ultrasonic sound transmission called "The Silent Sound Spread Spectrum (SSSS)," and sometimes called "S-quad" or "Squad." It was developed by Dr. Oliver Lowery of Norcross, Georgia, and is described in US Patent #5,159,703, "Silent Subliminal Presentation System," dated October 27, 1992. The abstract reads as follows:

"A silent communications system in which non aural carriers, in the very low or very high audio-frequency range or in the adjacent ultrasonic frequency spectrum are amplitude- or frequency-modulated with the desired intelligence and propagated acoustically or through vibrations, for inducement into the brain, typically through the use of loudspeakers, earphones, or piezoelectric transducers. The modulated carriers may be transmitted directly in real time or may be conveniently recorded and

---

[44] A sinusoidal wave form is based on the trigonometric sin function. Non-sinusoidal means not a sin wave. Typically, it might be trapezoidal, pulsed, square or a combination of these.

[45] Rantburg Gulf War I at www.qrmapps.com/gw1/day1.htm (accessed May 6, 2009)

stored on mechanical, magnetic, or optical media for delayed or repeated transmission to the listener."

This company has licensed the technology in Japan for use by automated soft drink vending machines. When a person passes in front of vending machines equipped with this technology, one inaudibly hears in one's head—that is, subliminally—the sound of ice cubes falling and clinking into a glass and the can of soda being opened with the characteristic pffft. Presumably this subtle and inaudible message encourages a passerby to consider buying a soft drink from the automated vending machine.

Some large department stores reputedly use ultrasonic sound transmission to hypnotically influence customers to pay for all their purchases. These hypnotic suggestions are used to reduce losses due to shoplifting. But, in theory, they also could be used to influence customer buying habits.

Some charismatic (Pentecostal) churches in the United States, as well as in some eastern European countries, have used ultrasonic subliminal suggestions to increase the "volunteer" donations of the believers as well as to create and strengthen belief in miracles. Perhaps this is the way a charismatic preacher can demonstrate that miraculous healings take place in his church.

Law enforcement districts in California have tested the use of ultrasonic sound with hypnotic suggestions for crowd control, suicides, hostage situations, traffic stops, and other situations. The results of these tests are not known, but presumably mind control techniques in this area are being refined. Once refined, you will find them in your own city.

While both ultrasonic and electronic trance creates hypnotic trance, this new method of delivery of suggestions is distinct and important enough to deserve specific treatment. Ultrasonic and electronic trance may well become much more common in the near future. We may be entering an age of subliminal mind warfare, in which governments, corporations, religions, and other groups compete to instill behaviors, performance, beliefs, and delusions that suit their specific agendas. Because this invasive form of hypnotic behavior modification is done without any prior knowledge or the consent of the target, it is a form of trance abuse. When competing suggestions occur, the result is likely to be confusion, depression, frustration, and anger—without knowing why.

Ultrasonic and electronic means of inducing trance work because the method of delivery does not allow critical judgment to operate normally. In other words, it is done subliminally, secretly, and surreptitiously. Invasive trance techniques represent opportunities for exploitation in which the victim is passive, uncomplaining, and acquiescent. It is like having someone come into your bedroom at night, sedating you with an ultrasonic/electronic device so that you fall into a deep trance, raping you, and stealing all your money. In the morning you don't feel right, you feel sore and all of your money is gone. You don't remember anything except you feel both strangely patriotic and singularly unmotivated to do anything about it. Depressed, in other words.

In the following paragraphs I will describe some of the current and potential methods and applications of sonic, ultrasonic, and electronic methods for inducing trance. Please note: I do not advocate the use of any of these pernicious forms of trance abuse. But it is important to present the scope of usage in such a way that you can easily understand some of the dangers of these methods of trance induction. By understanding and exposing the danger clearly, steps can be taken to contravene any of these methods. Also, by using a progressive typology of sonic, ultrasonic, electronic, non-invasive and invasive methods, you may begin to understand what the future may bring. In short, it will probably bring a combination of these delivery methods as well as use the structural typology I have set forth regarding meditation, hypnosis, addiction, and charisma. All of these techniques have a measurable wyrd, all have a great potential for transforming behavior without permission, and all will change your destiny as a person and as a citizen. If it is done in secret, then whether you agree to be manipulated or not is certainly not the point. It is only after you become aware of the outrageous thing that has been done to you that you might want to object in the strongest terms.

We first need to distinguish between sonic or audible means of creating a trance and ultrasonic and electronic (inaudible) forms of trance induction.

Audibly Induced Trance

An audibly induced trance is the easiest to spot because you can hear it. Your critical judgment is still intact, and unless it becomes disabled, you have a chance of avoiding the influence of any suggestions.

If someone comes up to you and makes suggestions using embedded commands,[46] these are audible suggestions. If your critical judgment is disabled, you could easily be induced into a trance. But if you can recognize embedded suggestions, you might be alert enough to nullify their effect.[47] Being aware of repetition and cognitive loops is also of help in avoiding trance abuse.

Non-invasive sonic (audible) trance induction, by definition, can be heard, and so you can avoid and walk away from it. You know it is happening and you can, so long as you are not induced into a trance, escape from it.

Any hypnotist or stage hypnotist or a skilled user of NLP[48] practices some form of a non-invasive sonic trance inducing technique.

Some other examples have been mentioned earlier, such as the trance-inducing aspects of music, etc. You can always walk away or turn off these forms of non-invasive trance induction techniques because your critical judgment is enabled; you still have your Will, and you can decide whether you wish to continue to listen or not.

There is a fine line between non-invasive and invasive trance induction.

---

[46] See the list at the end of the chapter on Hypnosis.
[47] A list of embedded commands is included at the end of this chapter.
[48] Neuro-Linguistic Programming

Invasive Audibly Induced Trance

There are some trance induction techniques that you can hear, but they are invasive and it is difficult to escape their influence. If you are on the telephone talking to your insurance company, you are captive inasmuch as you might need to talk to the other party. But what if the your insurance company either tries to sell you an unrelated product while you are on the phone with them, or even worse, starts promoting a religious or political agenda? It is out of context for your insurance transaction, yet there you are, in a way needing to listen to it and at least you can ignore it. Ignore it? If you tune it out, the message might influence you more easily.

Usually phone calls tend to stick to the subject, but there is a trend in automated telephone response systems to press the envelope by adding unsolicited offers or alerting you to alternative methods of communication with them or giving you information not asked for and not related to the purpose of your call. It is but a short step from perniciously adding embedded commands and unrelated promotions to such automated responses.

Movie theaters and DVDs often show advertisements or promotions before the main feature film. Since movie goers are captive in their seats, if such advertisements contain hypnotic suggestions, the technique would be an example of an invasive audibly induced trance.

Television

Television is, of course, the most common means of trance induction with social, economic, political, and commercial effects and applications. Technically, television induction is not an electronic trance, but it is invasive. A trance is induced by television images stimulating the primitive human brain. As the images are understood by your reptilian brain, various cognitive functions, such as critical judgment and short term memory, are disabled, and inner involvement is enhanced.

Television is a proven and effective device for changing buying habits and modifying social habits, customs, and beliefs of large populations. Situation comedies, soap operas, and even newscasts have all been exploited to promote social and political agendas, and even religious attitudes.

Television uses rapidly changing images to disable critical judgment through sensory overload, fear, and confusion induction techniques; then it uses visual imagery and audio to deliver suggestions. One trance inducing loop missing from television that prevents an even stronger trance from occurring is the immediate response feedback from the viewer to the program that is inducing the trance. This type of feedback is, however, present in computer-based and virtual reality devices.

Computers

Computers and computer-based games are much more effective in inducing stronger trances than television. Joy sticks, mouse, and keyboard inputs do provide limited feedback to the software, which can modify visual and aural stimuli to deepen trance. Most commercial computer games are designed for "entertainment" purposes. But what constitutes effective entertainment? When software designers deliberately seek to induce trance to enhance the thrill of the chase, for example, they may justify it as being more effective. But the potential for exploitation of computer games as trance-inducers carries with it the danger of games being used to promote other agendas[49] in the same way television has been used.

Virtual Reality

Virtual reality (VR) is an assembly of local sense stimulators and action receptors individually programmed by means of a computer. VR uses many sensory input and output actuators so that how a person responds to stimuli influences or controls how the program subsequently stimulates the participant. For example, VR can track eyeball movement, detect changes in galvanic skin response, body temperature, and muscle movement. VR not only

---

[49] Such as preparing children to become suicidal killers.

can provide visual and audible stimulation, but can create tactile pressures and textures, temperature variations on the skin, and even smells and pain. Unlike television or computers, VR is highly interactive and personal. How these inputs and responses are used depends only on the sophistication of the VR software and the input and output devices. Synesthesia or mapping one sense into another becomes easy to do with software.

Some applied uses of VR are highly realistic simulations, remote control of dangerous or toxic processes, space exploration, micro exploration, nano and clean room manufacturing, virtual meetings of remotely located persons, advanced learning simulations, advanced skill training in areas such as space exploration, military combat, and complex medical procedures, PTSD[50] desensitization, mind manipulation, psyops, and, of course, torture.[51]

Some civilian and commercial applications are highly realistic action games, including virtual sex. With virtual sex and computer controlled VR remote processing, you think you are only shaking the hand of that distant partner, yet why does shaking his hand produce such a silly smile on his face? These kinds of applications are on the horizon of VR.

VR is similar to television, but will be much more effective as a trance inducing mechanism, because of the interactive nature of the multiple hypnotic trance loops. Interactive VR has many more trance inducing loop possibilities than non-interactive television.

While television is a proven powerful manipulator of attitudes and beliefs, VR promises to be even more powerful because it captures more senses, articulates interactively, and can deliver suggestions the moment critical judgment is detected to be disabled.

Virtual reality devices also have a strong addictive potential, because the multiple loops may be sustained over a long time period. When monitored and positively controlled, one could expect permanent behavior modification, fixing of belief sys-

---

[50] Post-traumatic stress disorder.
[51] I'm not advocating any of these, merely noting their possibility.

tems, mitigation of inappropriate responses, and enhanced skill training. When used unmonitored or haphazardly, one could expect a potential increase of neurological and psychological pathologies, development of inappropriate and compulsive responses and behaviors, development of delusions, fantasies, and hallucinations. The potential exists for creating pathological monsters using VR. The promise also exists for VR to be used to enhance human sensitivities and to electronically create a deep meditation experience.

As with any trance system with a high potential for abuse, such as VR, the questions to ask are: who controls this device, what is their agenda, and do they have positive control over all side effects? Until these questions are definitively answered, VR remains too dangerous to contemplate.

Ultrasonic (inaudible) Trance

Ultrasonic sound is sound that is at a higher frequency than normally audible to humans. Normally, humans can hear sounds within a range of 100 to 12,500 Hertz (cycles per second). Sound waves below 100 Hz are often felt rather than heard. Sound waves above 12,500 Hz generally are not heard.

Sound waves that are within the normally audible frequency ranges of 500 to 3,500 Hz can be superimposed on or electronically mixed with an ultrasonic carrier of 15,000 Hz resulting in an inaudible signal, which ranges between 12,500 Hz and 18,500 Hz. This superimposition is done by frequency modulation of the ultrasonic carrier frequency.

The ultrasonic carrier waveform itself does not necessarily need to be a true sine wave, but may occur in other various waveforms including square, pulsed, and trapezoidal waveforms. Modified wave shapes—such as trapezoidal—have been found by experimentation to be more effective than sine waves for delivering subliminal content to humans.

The result of various configurations of audible sound modulation of higher frequency carrier waves of different shapes results in an ultrasonic sound, which is not audible in a normal way but nevertheless will be understood subliminally.

When ultrasonic sound carries repeated suggestions, trance will be induced in persons without their awareness of the content of those suggestions. This is, of course, a form of trance abuse. The suggestions are effective because the delivery of suggestions bypasses the normal filter of critical judgment. You can't censor the suggestions because you are not aware of them. What, then, can be a defense against this pernicious influence?

Decoding the Suggestions

If you are a clever electronic engineer, you may be able to design equipment to detect and demodulate ultrasonic hypnotic suggestions and to render them audible in real-time. The prospect of, on one side, clever engineers decoding subliminal suggestions and, on the other side, clever engineers designing yet more subtle ways to avoid detection and decoding points to the front lines of future mind control warfare. There have already been several detection avoidance cycles in military forms of mind control warfare. In the middle is the victim who is subject to a variety of subliminal trance inducing techniques, and who is less and less able to know for sure what the content of those suggestions may be.

Non-Invasive Ultrasonic Trance

Non-invasive ultrasonic trance does not exist except perhaps in some hypnotic tapes you can buy for changing smoking or overeating habits. What makes it non-invasive is that the purchaser agrees to submit to the effect of subliminally delivered suggestions. One could, theoretically, ask for a script of the hypnotic suggestions to have some assurance that those were the only suggestions being delivered.

Electronically Induced Trance

Electronics have a large potential for trance abuse. We are surrounded by electromagnetic waves constantly. There is no escape from them.

This form of trance is not the same as television hypnosis. Television distribution may involve radio frequency transmission methods, but the trance inducing aspect is dependent on the loop between the content of the images and the responses of the viewer.

An electronic trance is a trance that is induced by means of direct electrical stimulation. Electronic trance relies on direct electrical stimulation of the brain either by attachment of electrodes or by electromagnetic waves. The latter includes skull stimulation by microwaves.

Microwave and Ultrasonic Trance Induction

Pulses at microwave frequencies have been shown to be effective carriers of subliminal suggestions.

Microwaves have been used in military projects as an attempt to communicate directly with troops without normal telecommunication equipment.

This technique grew out of an observation by radar technicians that they could "hear" the radar signal in their heads. There were some experiments done on this phenomenon, and it was concluded that microwaves of very small power could be used to stimulate the brain directly so that audible signals could be heard directly. Here's the abstract of one experiment conducted as far back as 1962.

"The intent of this paper is to bring a new phenomena to the attention of physiologists. Using extremely low average power densities of electromagnetic energy, the perception of sounds was induced in normal and deaf humans. The effect was induced several hundred feet from the antenna the instant the transmitter was turned on, and is a function of carrier frequency and modulation. Attempts were made to match the sounds induced by electromagnetic energy and acoustic energy.

130

"The closest match occurred when the acoustic amplifier was driven by the RF transmitter's modulator. Peak power density is a critical factor and, with acoustic noise of approximately 80 db, a peak power density of approximately 275 mw/cm2 is needed to induce the perception at carrier frequencies 125 mc[52] and 1,310 mc. The average power density can be at RF as low as 400 μw/cm2. The evidence for the various positive sites of the electromagnetic energy sensor are discussed and locations peripheral to the cochlea are ruled out."[53]

The science underlying this technology is known to neurophysiologists, but not well known by the general public.[54] In some ways, the technology remains secret and the equipment used to produce such signals is considered to be war materiel.

When the signal transmitted is not audible—ultrasonic— then the equipment can be used by aircraft for propaganda purposes, without the knowledge or awareness of the population over which the aircraft flies.

Mind control conspiracy buffs and the paranoid will be delighted to speculate that US Aircraft flying overhead right now are broadcasting hypnotic suggestions to citizens in America so that they might more peacefully acquiesce to a dictatorship. The technology has existed since 1962. Powerful political groups with black ops[55] capability might be motivated to attempt control of the population in exactly that way. The US Military conducted foreign operations in Iraq using this technology in the 1980s. There is no hard evidence that it may be in use in America. It may be impossible to know for certain how much of our current social and political conditioning has or has not been influenced by the potential and presumed use of invasive trance control techniques in the United States and to what extent the use of these techniques could be responsible for current political apathy.

---

[52] mc was the abbreviation for megacycles, now MHz (megaHertz).

[53] Frey, Allan H., "Human Auditory system response to modulated electromagnetic energy." J. Appl. Physiol. 17(4): 689-692. 1962.

[54] Justesen, Don R., "Microwaves and Behavior." J. Am. Psych. Assn. 30(3) 1975

[55] Black Ops refers to the capacity to carry out a surreptitious and illegal action, such as burglary, assassination, etc.

Applications of invasive trance induction

There are many potential uses for invasive trance induction in medical, military, law enforcement, religious, and corporate venues. Here are some of the ways electronic or invasive trance induction techniques might be used in the near future—if they are not already being used. I do not advocate any of these applications, but I am aware that they may be used.

Medical Uses

Trance inducing techniques can be used in medical and surgical venues. Electronic trance—called "electro-sleep"—can be used to induce muscle relaxation and pain insensitivity sufficient for surgical procedures. Some dentists use hypnosis as their preferred method of anesthesia for minor dental repairs. Why not broadcast ultrasonic hypnotic suggestions in the dental office to soothe the anxieties of patients before they even sit in the dental chair? Indeed, hospital environments could be places in which such soothing suggestions electronically blanket large areas. Electronically induced trance could also be used to help patients recover more quickly and with fewer complications. However, it might be counter-productive since doctors and nurses would be affected as well.

Trance induced pain relief creates the delusion that the body is not signaling pain. Suppressing pain and anxiety may be psychologically helpful to medical personnel or family who cannot stand to see patients suffer, but eliminating a medical symptom is fundamentally not helpful and may bring a patient into even more danger.

Military Uses

Military organizations require obedience to orders. Electronic ultrasonic and invasive trances could be used as part of military training in order to produce soldiers who do not question orders. Or, as mentioned above, these trance techniques could be used as a military weapon against other armies or civilians.

Law Enforcement

Law enforcement can use trance in order to compel specific behaviors without the use of violent force. The cooperation of traffic offenders could be compelled by means of ultrasonic and or local microwave hypnotic suggestions. Those threatening suicide might be compelled to give up such desires. Hostage and terrorist situations may be brought to peaceful ends by means of ultrasonic hypnosis. In prisons where tension is high, ultrasonic suggestions could be used to promote peaceful cooperation.

Corporate Applications

Corporations may use ultrasonic hypnosis in order to compel purchases or to mediate shoplifting. What could enhance corporate profits better than to be able to create or tune consumer compulsions to buy products they don't necessarily need? One might argue that this is already effectively done with television. However, why continue to use old technology when a more effective technology is readily available today?

Social Control

Controlling populations effectively has been a subject of concern to various rulers and political systems for thousands of years. Many techniques have used fear. Others have used physical punishment and fear of that. More effective methods used religious indoctrination. Currently, social control techniques primarily involve the use of the television. Another, more modern technique would be the general broadcast of ultrasonic and microwave suggestions; they could help to influence social, moral, and sexual behavior and to limit political choice.

Belief Management

In the forefront of modern technological means of social control are a few religious institutions. Ultrasonic trance is known to have been used by some religious institutions in order to influence the rates and amounts of donations as well as to increase the belief in miracles. Behavioral modification is also in use.

The control of belief systems by means of ultrasonic and microwave induced suggestions has applications in the political arena as well.

Reading Thoughts and Recording Emotions

There is some research showing that it is possible to both read emotions as well as to send or broadcast them. After all, it is really not necessary that the content of an hypnotic suggestion be words. The content can also be a series of emotions played over and over again.

Mind Warfare

The big problem in invasive electronic and ultrasonic trance induction is that competing for the minds and even the souls of ordinary people may have deleterious effects and unknown consequences. Underneath the competition for minds is the questionable assumption that some sort of homogeneous mind set is socially, commercially, and ethically desirable and feasible. These issues raise profound ethical questions about the use of trance in this way.

Exercises

1. If you are an electronics engineer, build an electronic device that accepts audio and translates it into an ultrasonic form. Allow for various wave forms including sinusoidal, square, trapezoidal, and pulse. Construct an ultrasonic amplifier able to drive a Piezo transducer at the ultrasonic frequencies. Include a high-pass filter to reject frequencies below 12K Hz. Then build an electronic device that listens to free source ultrasonic audio content, demodulates the 15K Hz carrier, and produces an audible output suitable for recording.

2. Using some of the hypnotic induction techniques in this book or by purchasing hypnotic induction scripts from third party sources and with the electronic device from Exercise 1 are you able to influence the behavior of your friends and family so that, for example, they give up smoking or overeating?
3. What other ways can this technology be used in socially beneficial ways? What ethical questions are raised if this technology is used for beneficial purposes but without the informed consent of the people it is used on?
4. In what ways can this technology be abused? Which groups do you think are more likely to abuse this technology, and why?

Questions
1. Which carrier wave form for the device in Exercise 1 works best?
2. Discuss some possible applications of VR using ultrasonic trance techniques for reprogramming humans. Which is more likely: creating enlightened beings or creating monsters? Why?
3. Discuss the ethics of the trance abuse of Exercise 3.
4. Using the device in Exercise 2, are you able to discover and decode ultrasonic transmissions from other sources?
5. Why do you care about future mind control technology? Or why do you not care?

Ethics

The Twisty Little Passages of Trance

Trance raises some profound and serious ethical questions. It is important to understand, not only what a trance is, how it is created, how it may be terminated, but also in what ways it is used, whether with creative, beautiful, destructive, ugly, spiritual, dangerous, abusive, or lethal intent.

In this chapter, I will discuss these questions more to open a discussion and increase understanding rather than to provide absolute answers. No understanding of trance ethics can be complete without at least first examining the structure and history of trance and comparing what we find with our own personal experience. By making some observations and statements, I hope to expose and perhaps clarify some of the ethical questions that have come up along the way in my own investigation of trance.

Trance has a long history of use within common, ancient, and modern religious communities as well as by more peripheral shamans, charlatans, witches, hypnotists, alchemists, advertisers, politicians, and yogis. Because of this wide variety of uses of trance and the wide variety of motivations, purposes, objects, and victims involved, understanding the ethics of trance is vital, at least in order to help us distinguish a positive and supportive use of trance from a purposefully criminal use.

Trance has a built-in taboo in the sense that there is a part of the mechanism of trance which is, depends on, or becomes, secret. This mechanism is the fact that short-term memory becomes disabled soon after a trance is started, effectively creating a taboo. This taboo is an important characteristic of trance that gives the trance its power. It is also its most important characteristic that creates the ethical problem. Recognizing a trance is somewhat easy: the strongest evidence pointing to a trance is disabled short-term memory, disabled critical judgment, literalism, repetition, and denial. What is often not so easy to identify is the originator or creator of a trance, nor is it easy to fix attribution and determine method, motivation, and opportunity. If the power of voluntary choice is removed, in a hidden or secret way, from one person to another, an ethical problem is created.

Of course, not every trance is created for malevolent reasons. The use of trance by yogis, witches, alchemists, and shamans may have aided their understanding of the subtle energies of the planet as well as to help them to understand plants, animals, and human nature, and also, more profoundly, subtle intelligent entities and spiritual forces. Understanding the nature of these subtle energies, as well as experiencing them profoundly, from an illumination by trance may help many people overcome disease, grief, misfortune, or open their eyes to hidden knowledge. Doubtless, the positive uses of trance have helped society advance in many ways. And, no doubt, these positive effects have also helped people tolerate the taboo of trance to some extent. Understanding the wyrd energies of plants, insects, and animals can unlock potential medicinal and planetary healing properties, or it can unlock them as lethal poisons to be used for war, exploitation, and survival. If one uses trance to uncover hidden knowledge of some sort, there is a temptation to use this secret knowledge to exploit the ignorance of others. This starts to raise some ethical questions about the use of trance.

The use of trance in manipulative or abusive ways for darker reasons is, in the long term, very destructive. To know how to create a trance that one knows will be used in clearly abusive situations or destructive ways always creates social, legal, and ethical liability. The ethics here seem to be clear, but only because we know the purpose of a trance.

But what about the case in which the perpetrator uses the public ignorance of trance in order to deceive? Because trance creates dissociated conditions in which realities and perspectives change and egos split, one could try to avoid culpability of a criminal act by simply claiming that "It wasn't me, your Honor, t'was the Devil what made me do it." A judge might accept such a defense because of his poor understanding of trance. But a judge's inquiry into the mechanics and ethics of trance could expose a defendant's claim as resulting from either his poor understanding of trance or a deliberate criminal malfeasance.

Most hypnotists claim that you cannot be made to do anything by hypnotic treatment which you would not ordinarily permit. Presumably, this claim is intended to absolve a hypnotist of any legal responsibility if the perpetrator's defense of a criminal act was that "T'was the hypnotist what made me do it, your Honor."

Hypnosis can create irresistible compulsions in which suicide, murder, dependencies, manias, and phobias exist with a reality indistinguishable from what we might term a "normal" reality. The group suicides of Jim Jones, the Solar Temple, and others, demonstrate the tragic possibilities when trance becomes a medium for abuse. Indeed, trance is the process that creates, alters, and destroys realities. So, it is not at all true that a competent hypnotist cannot compel you to act against your own will and self-interest. If a hypnotist can compel you to give up smoking or lose weight, that same hypnotist could compel you to eat and drink yourself obese. While most competent and professional hypnotherapists act within the constraints of a Code of Ethics, not every trained and competent hypnotist is so constrained.

A trained and competent hypnotist might work for an advertising agency, for example. It is the hypnotist's job to act in the best interests of his employer, not you. There is no Code of Ethics in this case. An advertiser wants a consumer to compulsively buy his product. One can argue that effective advertising campaigns are nothing more than hypnotically induced compulsions. The ethical problem here is that a consumer is unaware that a hypnotic technique has been used to influence behavior so that the consumer acts automatically in the best interests of the advertiser and against his or her own interests. Some people call this exploitation or manipulation. I call it trance abuse.

Although trance is used by religious folks, trance itself is not exclusively religious. Trance does create dissociation, and the dissociated condition is populated with the Other (non-Self) but this is not necessarily religious. With trance, natural ways and events of this world become revealed as more subtle spirits and intelligences. Fire, earth, water, air, spirits, and many other objects can become either more or less than what they seem to be. Trance creates or illuminates an appearance of a more subtle reality in which we can appreciate the unity and the duality, but some subtle questions are raised about consciousness and who we are.

The study and practice of trance techniques also brings one directly into the problem of consciousness. As soon as you begin to meditate, you separate into two—dissociation. Abstractly, the Self separates the Other out of itself, and appreciates the Other as non-Self. The Self knows that this separation is an illusion created by a modification (disabling) of a cognitive function that attributes the "I," Ego, or Mine to specific projected cognitive objects. But the Self is also subject to the disabling of short-term memory and forgets that it caused the separation; the Self is also subject to the disabling of critical judgment and then cannot know how the Other was created. So, the Other gets an attribution of reality. The Other becomes real, or seems to be real, and seems to have an independent existence and consciousness. This magical process is fundamental to any trance, and there are many ways to say the same thing.

Using some religious symbols, we could restate the situation this metaphysical way: One symbolizes the Whole and Two symbolizes Separation. Two also symbolizes Knowledge because there is the Knower and the Known. The Two also symbolizes what is hidden or the taboo, while the One indicates a Unity of both Knowledge and Ignorance. One also symbolizes stability and non-movement, but Two symbolizes movement and even energy. Extending this idea to trance, the One is the Ego self-absorbed in Being, while the Two is the Witness in trance.

Do we live fundamentally alone or are we an integral part of this world and this reality? This is another fundamental question that is part of the discussion of the One and the Two. It is about wholeness and separation, unity and duality. It is about being fixed in stone, immovable, dead, or full of movement, flexibility, and life.

Are you separate from the world, from other people, animals, plants, and earth? Is there a "fence" or some kind of a taboo or barrier, between you and everything else? Or do you feel the pain of others? When a child dies in a war far away, can you feel your connection to that child, or has a trance killed your compassion, your empathy with that dead child? What is the nature of this taboo against our feeling the pain of the planet? What is it so difficult to acknowledge the pain and destruction of the environment? When I hear of such denials, I immediately think there is an addictive trance at work. What is the nature of these trances that are covered by taboo? These are not merely metaphysical questions. They have ethical implications and may motivate you to seek more information about the nature and function of trance you see around you.

Trance is a very interesting phenomena within this discussion of the One versus the Two. Trance is nothing without dissociation, which is Two, but at the same time, the narrowness of attention and the disabling of various cognitive functions symbolically implies that trance is the One, the immovable. This may have something to do with the idea that being in a trance is a divine act. As I have pointed out earlier, trance is scrambled up with religion, so many people believe that there is something "spooky" and "weird" or other worldly when someone has that fixed-eyed stare characteristic of trance.

By addressing or referring to these somewhat ancient metaphysical questions within the paradigm of the Trance Model, we may start to understand why trance is important as a way of discovering and using hidden knowledge. Our understanding will have implications in terms of law, knowledge, behavior, respect, and consciousness—as well as ethics. There are implications for celebration as well as ritual, whether we are talking about a trance party, using drugs, or leading a religious ceremony or a political movement.

Separation, Fences, and Dissociation

We are simultaneously both separate and part of the whole. Trance primarily creates separation; it creates taboo through the generating of a wyrd. It opens us to non-ordinary possibilities. In our normal awareness, the universe of non-ordinary possibilities is separated from us and taboo for energy and evolution reasons. What works is on one side of the fence, what doesn't work is excluded. But what is excluded is not always unworkable. Sometimes in the systems of our separated condition we need what we have excluded. Trance helps us to find what we have excluded and opens us to the possibility of change. Knowing how the wyrd works enables us to both build important fences for protection as well as to extend and scale our reach into the unknown or forbidden.

For example, if you become familiar with the internal worlds by practicing trance, you may learn how to see subtle energies. This familiarity can help you to avoid danger as well as how to become an aid for someone who is ill or in danger. Developing this perception over the years, you can even become a seer, a shaman or a healer—if that's what you want to be. Meditation and other trances helps you make the changes within yourself and enables you to jump the reality fence and go beyond the ordinary. What are your ethical responsibilities towards others if you gain skills through trance?

There is socially a resistance to change because people hate the unfamiliar, the strange. That resistance is symbolized by the fence.[56] The fence keeps out and also keeps in. If a fence is too small, we will begin to create loops, and the generated result of those loops is a kind of energy that will first make the reality within the fence the only reality. This is one of the early effects of trance: the creation of concentration. Another effect of a loop within the fence is to stir up the kind of energy that will break the fence or leap over it or draw in energy from outside the fence, ultimately weakening it. This is the way that change is created

---

[56] There are many other terms for "Fence": The Chasm, The Veil, barrier, etc.

and destiny is changed. Those who make societies' laws try to control if not suppress this second effect of the trance generating loop, but mostly, societies' law makers do not understand how trance works. Strangely, it is the very mechanism of control and limitation that creates the dynamic energy responsible for increasing the wyrd and causing the change. This is the secret dynamism of a fence or taboo. It is also the reason the yogi goes into a cave to meditate. In the cave the energy for change can be focused and concentrated. At some point the yogi must come out of the cave, because the energy (wyrd) for change is too much. The trance wyrd becomes tangible and active.

Compassion, Loving

The One creates the Two out of itself, and being a reflection of the One, generates both love and compassion in spite of the fact that the Two manifests the fence, the Veil, and the Chasm between life and death.

The Two manifests the One through Love. This has an important parallel in the trance model, because it is through the development of the strength of the wyrd from meditation, hypnosis, addiction, and charisma that trance gains enough power to change destiny. That is, the One manifests destiny through the creation of Two, but the Two—through the powerful creation and use of Devotion—manifests One. This changing of One into Two and Two into One comes about through the energy of the wyrd, and at this level the wyrd is extremely strong because it is creating the world. In some ways, we could say that the wyrd is like love or compassion because the creation loves the One and wants to return to it. No wonder meditation is at the root of creation! No wonder the evolved state of meditation is divine love!

Taboo and the Source of Secret Power

Why are there secrets? Why do we cover our genitals? Why are there separations between those who have power and those who do not have power? The inside of your cell phone is taboo;

you may never understand the technology. The operating room theater is taboo to the unwashed, profane, non-medical. What does the yogi do to make his magic? Whatever he does, it is done in secret, far away from people. Why is it that even if we are explicitly told an esoteric secret, we still don't get it? Taboo is taboo—and there is a fence you cannot cross. What is the meaning of a magical circle? Why is the craft of the witch taboo? Criminals work in secret; their activities are taboo to the law-abiding. The most important manufacturing processes are proprietary and covered by secrecy; the manufacturing facility is fenced; it is taboo to us consumers. Only within a taboo can the wyrd energy be created that changes destiny.

The same careful ethical considerations we apply in breeching the taboos of the above examples requires a full understanding of how trance works. Inside a taboo things are not what they seem. There are violations of rules, but that's what makes it work. We cannot apply the ethical standards of the One to the Two or vice versa, or the inside of the taboo to the outside. If we do, the wyrd stops; it becomes crazy nonsense. If the non-sterile unwashed pedestrian snoops inside the sterile operating theater, the operation will become infected and fail to produce the expected results. You may not breech this taboo, but you can work with it.

The Rejection of the Separation

Two lovers wish to be together. Taboo keeps them apart. When they breech the taboo, then they are together; their combined, shared, secret intimacy creates a taboo for others. Love is the force that manifests the creation. The mother loves her child and neither the mother nor the child wishes to be separate from the other. The fence which divides us each from the other is the fence of the skin and the artificiality of the ego saying: this is mine, as if the ego had an independent existence. The independent existence of the ego is an illusion shared by most of us, so we superficially accept the social illusion of possession and ownership rather than universal consciousness. In some ways, society and religion provide us with some methods of trance and intoxication to allow us to see the One behind the fence but not to realize it. Society and religion generally provide crippled ways to become One; if you are serious, you must go beyond the normal and reject the crippled ways of the ordinary experience and use trance to discover, use, and become universal consciousness.

Intoxication and the Divine Social Contract

"Divine" means "pertaining to God" in a typical popular sense, and in a more pagan way "soothsaying," but the word divine is very ancient. Looking at the word from another way, it could mean "from the vine" and as such implies, the intoxicated condition may have been associated with divine intervention of some sort. This non-standard interpretation of the word makes sense. An ancient and pagan view of the divine may refer to an intoxicated or altered state in which prognostication or divination could readily be accomplished. The oracle at Delphi had the help of an intoxicating gas to aid in her divinations. Some tribes have used corn beer celebrations to both honor the successful harvest of the past and to predict the future. Of course, the vine of choice in western traditions is the grape vine, but among natives of South America it may very well be *ayahuasca*.

Either way, it is probably unarguable that any grace from a natural god is bound to cause intoxication or a change in destiny at the very least. Thus, it is not a complete definition that divine merely pertains to the God. Rather divine refers to a specific characteristic of God: the intoxicating characteristic. We must be intoxicated—or blessed, some say—before we are transformed, before the wyrd changes our destiny.

Who are, after all, the so-called representatives of God on earth? Jesus, the local parish priest, the local Rabbi, the local Imam, Buddha, Mohammad, the Pope, Rinpoche, Ali? Here we come to a group of individuals who get their license to represent God by the severe duties of long term meditation. They speak in intoxicated tongues. They have the crazy wisdom. They perform miracles and raise the dead. What is it with these crazy people? Are they really intoxicated? Can a sacred life have something to do with being intoxicated?

A simple explanation of the divine is that it is a state like intoxication. It is a state that can be simulated by meditation or the consumption of magical liquors and potions such as naturally come about when a sugary corn or malt sits for a lunar month or which also come about from the incredible variety of plants or fungi on this planet that say Eat Me. Hindus drink their ganja milkshakes; priests drink their wine. I am arguing that so-called divine states are in fact trance-like intoxicated states, and that critical perspectives of one should be applied to the other as well in order to reveal hidden characteristics and similarities. Intoxication brings one to a place—very similar to meditation—in which there is a new understanding or revelation of the world. Why, then, is this particular trance-like intoxication suppressed by society?

Violence, Destruction, War, and Prisons

If intoxication separates man from the ordinary world, another type of "intoxication" separates man from mankind. The idea of "good versus evil" also produces separation and is the ontological source of violence, destruction, war, and prisons. The unitary state of consciousness means that there is neither good nor evil. Violence takes place due to the separation and delusion that the Other (non-Self) is evil. Destruction takes place when the object is not the self. War exists when there is no communication. Prisons warehouse those who are not connected with the others in society. These special forms of dissociation all perpetuate themselves like addictions. Such addictions can be broken and the delusions resulting from these social trances terminated.

They originate from the fundamental ignorance of not knowing where the "I" is when dissociated. It is the delusion that somehow the "I" (Witness or Self) is ontologically separated from the object of the trance (Other). Whatever is done as a hypnotic trance to increase the reality of the Other also works to create a taboo against knowing the real basis of the trance. The Other, which came into existence by the operation of consciousness (Self), is totally experienced by the Self as an independent, separately created and self-existing phenomena.

All fences created to keep the Other out further increases and guarantees the perpetuation of the delusion of the independent existence of the Other. This includes the perpetuation of ignorance, which is founded in non-communication with the Other. In other words, lock it up, don't communicate with whatever is beyond your fence, and you will guarantee for yourself an addicting experience of perpetual violence and war.

The same analysis applies to economic models. If any object becomes an Other (product) for which there is a fence (price in the commercial sense), you will guarantee an addiction that results in perpetual violence and war.

Trance and Democracy

Trance is a proven way to create delusions, belief system modification, false memories, and compulsions, both in individuals and on a mass scale. Populations and social groups can be convinced of the moral certitude of a wide variety of absurd beliefs, including the correctness of specific sexual customs and behaviors, social exclusivity, and marriage possibilities based on sexual, racial, or social membership; beliefs and delusions regarding one or another religion or political membership; and the ethical and moral rectitude of a variety of economic models, including slavery and less extreme economic models of exploitation. Groups in a trance can be convinced of their moral superiority while simultaneously committing all sorts of heinous crimes including torture, genocide, and even a belief in the efficacy of suicide. None of this has anything to do with democracy although voting and the free exchange of ideas seems puerile and naive when contrasted against the machinations of political system gamers.

The belief in the moral superiority of democracy is too often exploited by politicians for a variety of purposes including personal self-aggrandizement at fundamental odds with common ideas of democracy and the general promotion of the public good. When trance becomes a convenient tool for maintaining political power and personal profit, it is compulsively tempting for nefarious politicians to recklessly manipulate the populous belief in democracy to whatever ends suits them. Yet, merely prohibiting the use of trance by political criminals is hardly a promising prospect.

The argument that benign motivations of progressive politicians justify the use of trance in order to overcome the ignorant resistance of obstinate reactionaries is a poor justification for ignoring the critical value of education in a democracy. Trance might promote acquiescence, but education promises support.

Issues and Resource Management

Breaking an addiction to a delusion, in which the delusion is a product, a criminal, a water source, a sexual preference, an oil source, or the beliefs in favor of or against a particular terrorist group or state philosophy or religion is at least as difficult as breaking a life-long addiction to crack or heroin.

The simple answers have been known for thousands of years and ignored for at least as long. It starts with communication, education, gathering knowledge about the Other, and bringing the reality of the Other intimately close, so close that you can really feel love as opposed to either desire, repulsion, or fear. The basis of fear is ignorance; fear diminishes with communication. The effect of communication (rather than maintaining a fence) helps to break the addictive trance by modifying the sense or perception of the object. This, in turn, destabilizes the hypnotic trance and weakens the addiction.

So, for example, if the issue is a water source and competition for this resource has lead to violence and war, the first way to break the addiction is to communicate. Delusions about the water source itself might be cleared up by providing actual details about the water quality, water usage, water availability. Education and research involving new ways to use or conserve water and sharing this knowledge is also a way to lessen a fixation on a specific water source itself. This, over time, destabilizes the addictive aspect of the trance and helps to develop love and respect for life.

Many of the ideas raised above are not new in themselves but have been raised in the context of trance ethics and the Trance Model in order to demonstrate applications as well as to show some new perspectives or approaches to perennial problems.

Exercises

1. Think of something bad, criminal, or evil that you would like to do. Do you notice within yourself a limit or resistance to thinking in this way? What do you need to do in order to continue the thought? In some ways, your desire has become secret, taboo. Discuss the ethics of a meditation on evil in terms of the trance wyrd and taboo.
2. Should meditation or prayer ever be made illegal? Discuss the ethics of meditation in general.
3. What about music? Music makes a trance. Should music ever be made illegal?
4. Observe a plant or rock for one hour without trying to understand anything. At the end of the hour what changed? What is the effect of the wyrd or on the taboo of the rock? What is the ethical effect of your passive observation?

Questions

1. The suppressed Greek God Dionysus embodied the idea of triple birth, masks, lust, and intoxication. Discuss these ideas and trance ethics in relation to the religious suppression of Dionysus.
2. We all know how bad intoxication is. Assume intoxication is healing, and discuss how the moral opposition to intoxication has influenced the perception of trance. Discuss the intoxication taboo as really being a support of religious power. Find many examples.

3. Debate is an old democratic tool for elucidating issues and promoting new ideas. Discuss the ethics of and justify the conditions for the use of trance techniques in a debate.
4. "Give a man a fish and you feed him for a day; teach him to fish and you feed him for a lifetime" is an ethical statement promoting process over results. Discuss education and trance in these terms.
5. The United Nations and governments promote the control of drug, criminal, and terrorist activities through interdiction and repression. These methods are proved unsuccessful. Discuss the role that trance plays between addiction and evolution in the control of taboos.

Ecstasy

Dancing With The Gods

Now we consider the ecstatic trance or simply ecstasy.[57] This is not a distinct form of trance; an ecstatic trance is really just a complex trance. This is the type of ancient or so-called "primitive trance" we find throughout history and across many indigenous cultures in religious, social, and medical (healing) settings. We also find the ecstatic trance form in Balinese and African dances, Middle Eastern Sufi dervish dances, in the healing ceremonies of the Pacific islands, North and South American shamans, Caribbean Santeria, Voodoo, Obeah, Shango, Brazilian Macumba, and also in more modern music including the blues, jazz, rock and roll, spiritual and gospel music, reggae, as well as among the attendees of trance parties, Wiccan circles, and other celebratory tribal gatherings.

Ecstatic trance is used to experience the universality of the world; to make contact with subtle energies, spiritual entities; to obtain secret knowledge; to utilize and manage healing forces; and to utilize magical and hermetic processes resulting in personal transformation. Ecstatic trance is primarily a spiritual and mystical practice found more among ancient tribal and pagan religions than in traditional western religions. Whenever any religion is more concerned with guilt, dogma, and interpretive intercession than with direct, primary, personal spiritual experience and universal consciousness, ecstatic trance is very rare

---

[57] I want to emphasize that ecstasy as used here is not the empathogen Methylene Dioxy Meth-Amphetamine (MDMA) commonly known as Ecstasy.

and may even be feared and repressed. But the courage that is born of familiarity and trust values the direct, the natural, the unseen and is a light in darkness, which can guide the world through death and beyond.

Elements of ecstatic trance can be traced back at least to the ancient Greek Dionysus rituals, the practices of the ancient Tibetan Bö religion, or perhaps in even earlier, long vanished civilizations. As an example of the repression of ecstatic trance energies, Dionysus energies appeared to the Apollonian god to be somewhat dangerous or disturbing, so these practices and celebrations were—in the form of Bacchus—suppressed by the Romans and later more thoroughly by the Christian Inquisition. In spite of a repression that continues to this day—you can't kill a god any more than you can kill an idea—ecstasy and ecstatic trance regenerates and lives among isolated peoples and springs up occasionally and spontaneously like the spore of a magical fungus.

What is so disturbing to social order about the ecstatic trance, and what is its evolutionary function, if any?

Ecstasy opens itself up to chaos and reveals chaos ideally at the most profound and divine Brahmic level. From the point of view of Apollonian or Roman or Christian perspectives, this is the level of the uncontrollably insane, the crazy, the intoxicated. It is scary and dangerous because it is fundamentally unknowable, uncontrollable, and unpredictable. Even some meditation forms can bring up unusual thoughts. When coupled with addictive trance, unusual thoughts can result in delusions. The trancelings of such unhinged, ungrounded meditation practices can eventually result in permanent psychosis. If that happens, you know for certain you made some big errors. Ecstatic trance can be even more dangerous because results can occur suddenly. But ecstatic trance—in opening up to chaos—allows maximum creativity and helps in the evolution of humans by maximizing potential choices and selection possibilities. But fully manifested, chaotic energies can lead to lethal results, and to the profound destruction of any social order. Dionysian chaotic energies are not merely an open expression of life, of free

151

lust, but the same energies can also include blood and human sacrifice and even cannibalism.

In the previous chapter, we looked at trance ethics, because mind control and mind warfare encourages an extreme kind of social and legal chaos of the elite, which also threatens the social order though extreme control including a trance-based mental domination. Ecstatic trance potentially goes to the extreme in another direction. As we move along this theoretical continuum of trance from extreme mental domination towards ecstasy, we enter a situation where anything goes, and we are taken beyond the ordinary limits of mind, society, and sanity. Because these limits are both frightening and dangerous to most people, we must have at least a profound awareness of ethical balance before fully embarking in an ecstatic trance. We prefer not to suppress anything interesting that comes from an ecstatic trance, but to always keep aware of our balance as we get closer to the edge.[58]

Within the chaotic energies of ecstatic trance there is always a potential for self-destruction, and perhaps this is the fundamental reason for anti-Dionysus forces. Wild chaos and Dionysus ecstasy can really appear to be a threat to authorities who usually do not understand the function of this powerful and magical evolutionary[59] energy and perceive it wholly, and only, as a threat to the current "Roman" order. Or perhaps the authorities understand it all too well and are simply terrified of it and the possibilities it may bring.

Finding a balance to these primordial chaotic forces so that they add to evolutionary forces is a step on the way of trance. Here we find difficult and profound questions perhaps more suitable for an occult debating society. But without making moral judgments here, we can describe what is meant by ecstatic trance and explore some of the implications.

---

[58] Setting strict time and space limits helps to control the chaos and helps to maintain a balance with sanity. Fail-safe is good.

[59] Some people and institutions especially fear Dionysus energy because of it threatens to expose the limitations and fundamental falsehood of dogma. Many people have suffered and died because of these irrational fears. Be careful not to stir it up.

A Definition of Ecstatic Trance

An ecstatic trance is always created by a sustained hypnotic trance on or by a high number of meditation and hypnotic trance loops. The hypnotic trance can be created initially by highly repetitive (trance) music. The subsequent additional meditation and hypnotic trance loops can take the form of highly repetitive dance or physical movements, but may also be mental. Multiple visual, emotional, and other internal and external loops are created on or within the musical and dance trances that combine over time to create additional multiple complex trances. Ecstasy develops when the sustained interaction of the large number of meditation and hypnotic trances produces a chaotic effulgence or self-replication of multiple trance loops. Subjectively, anything is possible as the multiplication of different trance realities create something like a psychedelic universe. Or is this a tapping into universal consciousness?

The Structure

An ecstatic trance is composed of multiple meditation trance loops each with very few cognitive objects. The openness of ecstasy implies that every sensation, every feeling, every cognitive object is permitted, without censorship, and allowed to associate with any other cognitive object. The domain and range of critical functions expands as the cohesiveness of association is lowered. What becomes chaotic about it is the willingness of the mind system to allow multiple dissociations to start without trying to control them. Or the trance seems to be like a wave of light or gentle control, changing from one meditation trance to another, without trying to stop one before starting another. There is no self-awareness, no analysis, only flow. In this way, over a period of several minutes or hours,[60] multiple trances are created. Because each thought or sensation can itself begin a trance, multiple trances are created. For trance parties, the

---

[60] Who knows? Time distortion is commonplace.

music may be the greater influence in creating trance, but also the dancing and meditation contribute as well. The visual and tactile stimulation of the venue add additional trances. These all, when sustained over a period of time, create an apparent61 form of chaos, which is the ecstatic trance.

The Disabled Cognitive Functions

While in an ecstatic trance there will be a very large variety of cognitive functions being disabled and enabled, especially one right after another, or added to other cognitive functions. This chaotic combination can produce all sorts of new ideas, sensations, feelings, visualizations, and so on. Feelings of oneness, telepathic experiences, clairvoyance, heightened sensations of both the inner and outer worlds can become common and shared. The subtle is magnified. Delusions and hallucinations can also be present. Waves of new perspectives can produce global changes in beliefs, perspectives, and so on. The common and shared energies can also manifest in the abatement of individual disease processes, thus the ecstatic trance may have healing properties. Is this the universal consciousness we seek or is it merely another delusion resulting from the effects of a complex trance? Is there really a difference?

While one goal of disabling cognitive functions is to defeat the censorship of new, evolutionary possibilities, the fear which this type of cognitive deconstruction produces could drive a person to attempt to suppress the ecstasy—rather than the censorship—by means of drugs, alcohol, etc. The basis of fear is always ignorance; facing and going into the fear produces knowledge of it. Knowledge of the source of fear transfers courageous power to the knower.[62]

---

[61] It is apparent in the sense that a fractal or interfering sound waves can appear chaotic in the close-up details, but create apparent patterns from a more universal perspective.

[62] If it is of any encouragement, I have usually found that fears are not as powerful as initially apprehended; just a little bit of courage—long enough to look for knowledge and ask serious questions about the basis of the fear—is enough to vanquish the fear.

The Wyrd

Because the wyrd consists of the sum of the trances, ecstatic trance develops relatively strong wyrds especially when the trance is maintained for long periods of time. I suppose that very long ecstatic trances, such as for weeks at a time, would develop very intense results, especially if some of the deeper meditation elements of the trance are maintained and empowered by taboo. The wyrd grows according to the log of the duration of the trance; this means that sustaining an ecstatic trance for very long times would not appreciably increase the wyrd, that is, the change in the wyrd maintained for two weeks as opposed to one week would not be that profound.

Increasing the ecstatic trance wyrd by the use of taboo, means that the gathering—such as it is—is covered or limited or focused and protected. There are many ways to do this, from letting the trance party happen within a physical fence or magical barrier of some sort; to individual protection by means of string, bark, incense, special clothing; to local protections such as special altar, or places where continuous invocations are done. Specially made images of art can work as carriers of taboo. Presumably, powerful talismans can be created according to astrological precepts and include human, animal, and plant parts. I can see that the Trance Model could form the theoretical basis for the re-creation of all sorts of ancient ways previously lost. Do we want to go there? Shall we re-create the lost religions of Atlantis or Bö? Is this the way to re-discover universal consciousness? I am not sure.

While ecstatic trance can be a continuous process, human celebration is not. Ecstatic trance may give us a glimpse of the ethereal numinous, but celebration is always human and limited. Trance is one effective way we could move celebration into the numinous realms, but humans of the modern era do not generally allow this to happen, arguably for good reasons, but also perhaps for ignorant and fearful reasons.

Celebration

Why do we celebrate? What are we really doing when we have so much fun? Is there a reason why trance and party are connected? A celebration is used most often to mark the end of something or to mark a change. Celebration embodies the idea of sacrifice in the fact that we must say goodbye to the past, to our old fears and ego, and welcome new magical energy.

When a celebration is a form of ritual magic in which banishment and invocation are a formal and conscious part of the celebration, a celebration may be full of the kind of energy most often associated with chaos. That is, without banishing certain forms of negativity, the old and fearful first, we may be permitting them to re-manifest. Invoking the ancient and wise is not the same as neglectfully allowing the old and fearful.

Even a simple birthday party can become a form of ritual magic if you apply the principles of ecstatic trance.

There is a potential connection to alternative realities within a celebration, an invitation to other potentials or even numinous beings to come and make their mark on this reality. Expressed in this way, you may understand how a celebration, a party, can take on meanings that go way beyond merely invoking "TGIF," popping a cork, and playing loud music. Thinking about this deeper meaning of celebration is important if you want to pay more attention to the fundamentals of celebration and in so doing make your celebration more profound and move it towards ecstasy, the magical.

Seemingly unrelated ideas are related through the idea of the wyrd, the energy that changes destiny and is both created by and controlled by trance. Carefully looking at the trance structure, you can use the wyrd and the taboo to design effective magical positive parties and celebrations.

Sacrifice of the Self

Under the entire canopy of life, there is always change, for we live in time. By the action of trance, this world takes on the idea that it is permanent. Everyone in this world believes, through the action of trance, that the ego is permanent. Yet, we change. We are born, go to school, get up everyday to a new day, enjoy our new lovers and friends, and experience the departure of each and every day, as well as our friends and family to the realm of memories and ancestors. Even what we have learned in school is not permanent, because social, business, and economic needs and our values and beliefs also change. So, depending on how much we have meditated, we get used to saying goodbye to the ego, letting go of thoughts, and sacrificing what seems to be our self, our values, our memories, our health, our friends, our families, and our life. And all of these sacrifices, not always without some pain, are sometimes celebrated in a ritual, a party, an intoxication, a prayer, or a meditation. A celebration is secretly about the sacrifice of the self. It is about opening yourself to a change in your destiny including your own death. Taken to an extreme using trance techniques, celebration borders on, becomes the primordial ecstasy born of chaos. It is Dionysus energy reborn and re-manifested.

Transforming Ourselves

How wonderful is music when it puts you into a trance. Isn't the greatest art any art that entrances? And dance! The moving, twisting, and twirling in rhythmic patterns can propel you to other dimensions. These are all subjective descriptions of the effect of trance in music, art, and dance. That is the fun part of trance but also the very interesting part. In doing music, art, and dance, we actually don't need to understand what we are doing. But if we are creating music, art, or dance, an understanding of the trance aspects can increase our skill and efficiency in creating fun for others—to say nothing of the fun for ourselves.

The Trance Model offers a new perspective in the analysis of music and art. It is certainly not a traditional method of analysis, yet the fact is that much of our culture is expressing itself through technology, like it or not. So, an analytical methodology might be appropriate for these times. Another perspective perhaps is this is the end of modernity and we need to rediscover the ancient roots of Isis and Gaia. But for this perspective too we need to have an understanding of trance. It can be a practical understanding formed of many years of meditation and inner experience. The Trance Model can also be beneficial as a special tool for understanding and relating to those ancient roots while you dance, party, celebrate, or meditate.

Music, art, and dance, as well as meditation, all have repetition in common. It is the existence of repetition in these art forms that allows the Trance Model to be applied. Experiencing music, art, or dance either as its creator or as an observer always produces trance to a greater or lesser degree. The Trance Model avers a causal connection between repetition and dissociation. While this idea of a relationship between repetition and dissociation is not new, if applied consistently, the concept has important implications for music, art, and dance. These ideas will be discussed in greater detail below.

Music, art, and dance have been part of the human experience since the beginning. They have occupied important positions in social and religious celebrations and have fascinated scholars and philosophers for millennia. The creation and recognition of patterns in the arts is a source of joy for researchers as well as for artists. Carl Jung, like many other researchers, was fascinated by the repetition of themes, which he termed archetypes, expressing themselves spontaneously in the human psyche. Philosophers such as Santayana, Bertrand Russell, and others have all noted that the arts and especially the "great" arts have the power to remove us from the drab and commonplace into the magical world of the transcendent. The power of art to transform the commonplace into the magical, mysterious, and transcendent is an effect of an artist's efficient use of the wyrd in these artistic trance forms.

Technically, any repetition of elements or themes in art creates a trance generating loop. The trance that occurs is often experienced as self-reflection, self-observation, sometimes boredom, and sometimes creates literalism as well as the effects of any combination of disabled cognitive functions. These multiple effects, common in art-based trances, can also create so-called "religious experiences" along with heightened inner involvement and vivid inner perception. Such art can also mitigate physical pain, produce short-term memory loss, cause deep relaxation, pleasurable feelings, and create many other effects common to trance. In extreme cases, trance in art produces profound somatic and psychic changes, which are similar to the effects of orgasm or drugs.

What is "great" art but the efficient creation of trance with strong wyrds for the greatest number of people? How "great" a specific example of art may be is directly related to the strength of the wyrd created by the artistic trance. The Trance Model provides us with a new analytical methodology for the analysis of art as well as its creation.

Successful art does not consist of single themes and certainly does not consist of single trance generating loops. But fascination with art is an effect of trance: usually it consists of heightened creative visualization, suspension of critical judgment, reduction of bodily awareness, increased inner absorption, and so on. This is precisely what many people would call "hypnosis," but which I term here the more generic and more precisely defined trance. Successful art often embodies multiple themes, multiple trance generating loops, and many secondary trance loops so that the observer goes from one mini-trance to another: one trance is created, then is destroyed and another takes its place. These types of trances—in which trances are created and destroyed—are characteristic of both hypnotic and addictive trances. This modulation of the dissociated trance plane is one of the reasons we feel pleasure when we experience art.

If we, as artists, learn to excel as trance virtuosos, it becomes possible to create or play these mini-trances like an instrument through the medium of our art thus creating grand orchestral suites of trance inducing experiences. This is not a mechanical activity, and there is certainly no one way to create these kinds of grand artistic trances. But understanding the practical mechanics of trance may help you to create more powerful and more enjoyable trance effects with your art.

Modification of Destiny

Great music, art, and dance are all ways that induce trance and consequently modify the destiny of the observer. While this seems like a strong statement, it is not if you consider how your destiny is determined. I assume that if you do not make any changes, then your destiny remains the same. When changes are made in the way you process information, or how you make decisions, or what you observe and learn, then as a result you usually make changes in your life, and that means that your destiny changes. Of course, there are other ways in which your destiny may change, for example by accident or disease. But it can be argued as well that large changes in destiny can be attributed to many small changes in how you process information, or make decisions, or what you observe, or fail to observe. Failing to observe a stop sign, for example, can have fatal consequences. This is an example of a big change in your destiny caused by a slight change in perception.

Great art exemplifies the way trance can create almost compulsive changes in destiny. The trance wyrd is strong and alters cognitive functions on a mass social scale leading to new cultural values and potentially to social changes. The fugues of Bach, the art of Michelangelo, the ancient Hellenic Dianic religious dances, as well as the music of the Beatles and the Rolling Stones are some of the artistic examples of trances that have created powerful changes in western society. Lesser "great" art does not always create a change in destiny; sometimes art merely promotes a momentary intoxication or a slight modification of some cognitive functions, or it may merely produce slight dissociative effects subjectively perceived as boredom. But even boredom is evidence of a light trance and boredom can produce inattention long enough to render the subject suggestible or promote the acceptance of change.

Now we will look at three major categories of art: music, dance, and visual art. But we will examine them from the perspective of ethics and of trance.

Music

Music embodies rhythm and repetition. Is it any wonder that all music is intoxicating? We have already observed that repetition is the foundation of trance. Music is well-known as a producer of trance and its concomitant intoxicating effects. If the music is not so good, we get bored—also a trance. If the music engages us, we may spend hours deep in a reverie, a day dream, or be transported to unknown worlds. You can say that music was intoxicating, almost divine, and argue the effects of music until the early morning. Repetition in music is responsible for many of its effects. In other words, music always creates a trance and that is its primary purpose. Most people then ask, what kind of a trance is associated with a specific music and how strong can the associated wyrd become?

If music is intoxicating when experienced alone, how much more intoxicating is music when dance is added? And what about a light show? And what about strongly amplified rhythms that blast the body in physiological ways massaging the internal organs from the bottoms of your bare feet to the brains in your head? And what about the added effects of intoxicating smells, art, drugs and so on? Multiple applications of the causes of trance will produce strong trances, strong wyrds, and definitely change your destiny. So far as music can be secret or covered or talismanic, the wyrd in music can become taboo, and thereby more focused. Trance is not less than an alchemical transformative process.

And we have not even suggested here how the possible addition of ultrasonic and microwave stimulation might even enhance the trance effect even more. And let us not go into virtual reality setups or ritual magic. For if we did add additional trance technologies to a party, such a musical event would be very powerful indeed, which is to say, the trance wyrd would become compulsive and could bring with it considerable social and legal responsibilities.

If the idea of celebration and transformation is to make a wyrd strong enough to change destiny, then there are plenty of examples from all over the world as to the general social experimentation to increase the wyrd that has gone on for centuries. If we look at historical and sociological events as examples of trance, we come to an understanding of history that may have a new perspective.

Following the torches as they dipped and swayed in the darkness, they climbed mountain paths with head thrown back and eyes glazed, dancing to the beat of the drum that stirred their blood (or they "staggered drunkenly with what was known as the Dionysus gait"). In this state of ekstasis or enthusiasmos, they abandoned themselves, dancing wildly and shouting "Euoi!" (the god's name) and at that moment of intense rapture became identified with the god himself. They became filled with his spirit and acquired divine powers. [63]

The idea that culture is transmitted through music and poetry over centuries is easy to understand if it is the music and poetry that creates a trance, rendering the listener able to visualize easier as well as suspend critical judgment and short term memory in order to create ego involvement with the story and to identify with it. Musicians in the African kingdoms, which developed from the tenth century and extended for over a thousand years, served as the historians of their cultures. For example, in western Africa today, the Mande people recount in song and poetry the stories of earlier powerful families and in so doing advise their contemporaries. It is also well known that such songs and poetry are the medium for cultural knowledge and values. The community and society celebrate births, adolescent initiation rites, marriages, title-taking award ceremonies, funerals, and for the memory of ancestors—in short, all of the important events that mark a change in the destiny of a person's life.

In Africa, India, Bali, and many other places, the endless repetitions, prolonged sounds, rhythms all seem to the casual observer as primitive and monotonous, but as soon as one gets into the feel of it, a hypnotic trance develops in which deep inner exploration becomes possible. If there are words or lyrics or sto-

---

[63] Peter Hoyle, Delphi (London: 1967), p. 76.

ries, then these vocalizations work as suggestions to the trance which has developed a decrease in critical judgment, a decrease in short term memory, an increase of inner involvement, constructive visualizations, and so on.

The people of Asia and Africa are not unique in regards to the use of trance in music to produce celebration and transformation. The music of the early sixties such as Terry Riley, Steve Reich, La Monte Young, Phil Glass, Robert Moran, Frederick Rzewski, and many others experimented with the trance producing effect of endless repetitions; prolonged sounds; sustained notes and the production of their overtones; continuously repeated short, melodic motif-like figures; minimally varying polyphonic rhythms; and music constantly regenerated and sustained. What do these techniques do? They all create a trance in which heightened inner involvement can produce a suspension of critical judgment, disabled short term memory, constructive visualization, synesthesia, and even hallucinations. The sounds can appear "iridescent," they can transport the listeners to "other worlds," and they can open communications with the "spiritual world." But this borders on a religious experience, doesn't it? Certain kinds of music create trance and out of the trance comes a potential religious or spiritual experience. Which trance inducing techniques are best for producing ecstasy? Are there combinations of trances that can produce "universal consciousness?" Many producers of music seem to feel the answer is in the details of musical technology, the beats, the frequencies, the lyrics, the patterns of phrases. We can use the Trance Model even at this level to give us another perspective.

Beats per Minute

It is generally suspected that some beats may be more "effective" than others for inducing trance. Possibly certain ranges will in some people disable certain cognitive functions before others are disabled. Thus there would be some differences in the types of ASCs produced. Everyone is a little different, so I am not so certain that everyone would react the same way to a specific beat.

Ecstatic trance forms out of so many different approaches: techno beats, new tribes forming with new codes and languages, out of zeros and ones, electronic pattern forming devices, "Edutainment," inner peace through pounding club systems, and sensory deprivation, within concrete mazes, underground caverns. Subjectively, you're in an altered state, you've relinquished control of something and it feels great. You don't have to feel bad about life, just responsible for making the future a more enjoyable place to be, and you're not the only human that feels the same way. The collective feeling of the trance state is probably akin to Colin Wilson's description of early societies: the ability for individuals to think and act as one in the same way that a flock of birds move in formation. The mechanics of this shift in modern times are known to most clubbers or festival goers: drums/repetitive beats, lights/colors (to feel our photovore brains), sleep deprivation, and food choice—by which I mean anything we choose to imbibe. If enough minds and bodies agree to do the same thing, the collective reality of those involved can be changed or a new one created.

It has been argued that everyone is in one form of trance state or another, and many of us are imprisoned in types of repetitive behavior and thought, that if we had the option, we would escape from it. Cleaning out the cobwebs/breaking down the barriers between people every so often is pretty essential to our well being. When we are in a euphoric state, we wonder—how is it possible for us to all feel so different and isolated at one point and yet connected the next?

Sharply focused mental activity means brainwaves of all frequencies (desynchronized activity). Non-focused mental attention leads to an increase in alpha wave activity. This is what causes the interesting trance-like stuff and releases us from the bombarded ego that is Western adulthood. If you've taken a substance that makes all your neurons fire, keeping simple time to a 4-4 beat will be a mirror of this Alpha state. Many at trance parties report similar experiences.

If you want a natural effect listen to polyrhythms: drum circles, African rhythms, Tibetan music, and Moroccan music. The chaotic quality of the shifting natural patterns confuses the brain—as it tries to find the "correct" timing—we decipher our own "beat" within it, the action of doing this forms the non-focused, attentive mental state that stimulates Alpha wave activity.

Frequency

The other "turn-on" with sound is frequency. This is where the "chakra" idea comes into it. Bass most strongly affects the lower nerve centers—sexual organs and the stomach. Midrange affects the chest—particularly the heart rate—faster kick drums can affect the heart and thus manipulate adrenaline levels. Top end and white noise have most effects on the head/brain—as do piercing acid squeals. And the rest of it—melody, chord progressions, scales, the human voice? These are what influence our more subtle emotional responses, which are highly varied. To misquote Terence McKenna:

> "we have more words to describe narcotics than we do our emotions." And they seem to be one of the key areas of development of our species.

> "Any move to a permanent higher consciousness would require greater emotional capacity and understanding of inner rhythms via biofeedback techniques. These techniques enable conscious manipulation of brainwave and body function. This is why people are exploring group trance states in time and space at this period in human evolution."

Playing a CD or sample over and over again does produce a hypnotic trance—if the CD is sufficiently repetitive. But whether you filter or not depends on which cognitive functions remain enabled and which disabled after the trance is produced. The idea of using external stimulation, such as music on a CD, is precisely to artificially create enough stimulation to keep some of the interesting cognitive functions enabled while the repetition of the music induces trance. This balance between stimulation and trance can be achieved by mixing meditation with a repeating CD.

Dissonance

On the average, dissonance tends to shock and to break trance.

By this I mean that cognitive functions that have been disabled are pulled back into service. Dissonance sometimes will make a person aware of his body since dissonance can have a tension or stress producing reaction in the body. If a person is in a trance in which he is not aware of his body, dissonance in this case can create a tension in the body somewhere, which causes body awareness to increase. This requires energy, so the trance is terminated.

Lyrics and Rhymes

Positive suggestions work better than negative ones. If you are in trance and your rationality is shut off, you have a better than average chance of putting your listeners into trance too, because you are encouraging them to shut off their own rationality in order to find meaning in your lyrics. Repetition and rhyme is very important too.

Rhyming words set up other types of trance generating loops, which can be very useful in creating trance.

If the alchemical language you use does not have referents that your listeners can relate to, then better not use them. Nursery rhymes are okay, but even better is to use snips of nursery rhymes or a few notes of a nursery rhyme song.

The word "remember" is a powerful trigger word. The word has a lot of abstract, mystical associations and is quite magical. You can put yourself in a trance by "remembering" and remembering to remember . . .

Drumming obviously creates trance. Drumming provides a good demonstration of how trance theory works. The repeated beats always create a trance. The same rhythm loop(1) makes one trance(1). Another rhythm loop(2) makes another trance(2).

And so on. Drum beats that change loop(3), which creates another trance(3). Layers of rhythm loops in this way are very reliable ways to create a trance. Moroccan, African, and drummers all over the world know this.

All music is analyzable right down to the finest levels (if you are into analyzing) and gives clues as to what is creating the trance, and therefore, how it is possible to change what the drummer does to make better trances—or even to create trances for a "purpose" such as healing or normalizing biological functions or becoming sensitive to "other" energies/entities.

Words in Music

The general description of the process is: Repeated themes in music will always induce a trance. Trance results in disabling of some cognitive functions. The disabling of specific cognitive functions will allow "speaking in tongues," etc.

The content of the words used in gospel music should be analyzed for embedded commands. It may be that embedded commands are responsible for the construction of a prior trance, which is used subsequently.

If you follow what I mean, a primary trance is first constructed over a period of time, then a second trance is constructed on that with the loop of the second trance occurring in the dissociated trance plane of the primary trance. This is the basic structure of what I term an "addictive trance."

In this form of trance, the repeated musical themes or the repeated verbal suggestions occur in a preexisting dissociated trance and is further stimulated by music, song, or suggestions from the charismatic preacher. This is perceived from a second dissociated trance plane. This structure is similar to a bipolar frame found in some "schizophrenics" but is not necessarily pathological, although it could be. This is also the structure for an addictive trance and is probably found in charismatic churches. It allows for a kind of "post-hypnotic" type of action or action which seems to be automatic or involuntary. It may be connected with catharsis of some sort or what some might term an hysterical and emotional release. This release is falsely attributed to "spirit" and can result in bizarre behavior including laughing, crying, speaking in tongues, rolling on the floor, convulsions, and so on.

There are no unusual characteristics of any music, per se, which induce trance, but rather the other aspects of the situation take advantage of the "ordinary" trance that is created by the music. There are actually two (or more) trances created, but the main characteristic is that the second trance (or trances) is created with a loop in the dissociated trance plane of the primary trance (or trances) with a continuous stimulation from (probably) the preacher. Or it might even be in the words to the gospel music too, or in some combination that disables some inhibiting cognitive functions.

No music will take the place of meditation, and the effect of any music will be hypnotic trance inducing in general, which might not be what you want specifically.

Musicians who play music while or because they themselves are in a trance is probably the best. I would tend to avoid vocals or singing. Probably something primitive like drum and bass trance could have some of the effects you might want.

Repetitive, simple, and slow rhythms played with low light or candle light may help produce some of the effects you want.

Chanting

Chanting is defined as the rhythmic repetition of words or sounds and includes singing and the recitation of poetry.

Because chanting involves voicing sound, it is somatic and aural.

Because chanting is a repetition of elements, the elements (words) can be counted and they belong to a limited set. The words are the trance generating loop.

When the chant is learned and repeated several times, consciousness dissociates into the automaton consciousness, which repeats the chant, and to a second awareness process. The automaton consciousness is cognitive disabled. The second awareness is somatic disabled so far as voicing sounds is concerned.

Part of the available somatic energy is used to maintain the chant, and part of the cognitive energy is used to maintain the automaton, the trance generating loop. The remaining somatic energy may become insufficient to maintain somatic awareness, and some anesthesia may be present. The remaining cognitive energy may become insufficient to maintain some cognitive functions (such as attention and or judgment), and what may appear to be suggestibility may be present. If the content of the chant contains embedded hypnotic suggestions, in those cases that there is a disabling of judgment and volition there will be an increase in the trance wyrd with the result that the hypnotic suggestions will be carried out.

Let's look at a couple of other ways chanting induces trance. The Greeks used a rhetorical device called epanodos which means "the road back." With epanodos the pattern to say is: "a is b and b is a" like Shakespeare's "fair is foul and foul is fair." The trance generating loop is "Fair is foul." The second repetition of the trance generating loop is in a reverse order. The reverse trance generating loop is similar (and short) enough so that when the second reversed trance generating loop is completed, a comparison with the primary residual awareness begins. "Comparison" in this instance is the beginning of multiprocessing. The residual awareness is larger in the reversed paradigm of epanodos than the residual awareness of a simple multiple repetition of the trance generating loop, so epanodos would be a relatively effective device for inducing trance.

Another Greek rhetorical device also effective for inducing trance is the epistrophe. In this paradigm a phrase ends with the same term. This paradigm can be used in a classical hypnotic induction, for example:

As you sit in the chair, you close your eyes.

As you look at me, you close your eyes.

As you relax deeper, you close your eyes.

As you try to move, you close your eyes.

The trance generating loop in this case is the repetition of a epistrophic pattern terminating with "you close your eyes." Again, as the mind hears one phrase similar to a prior phrase, a mental comparison is made. The operation of memory in the comparison mode amplifies the residual awareness and causes dissociation. After some repetitions the awareness will be cognitive disabled in the dissociated trance plane in a trance and the trance generating loop will be "you close your eyes."

Most religious groups, from the Hari Krishnas to the Catholic, Buddhist, Jewish, Hindu, and Muslim monks and devotees, all use chanting as part of their devotional practices. When it is understood how trances are generated, it may be realized that there is nothing magical in chanting. But there could be significant or magical content in the words of specific chants.

Exercises

1. Use a drum or djembe. Begin to play a rhythm you can easily sustain. After several measures, begin to meditate using a mantra. Close your eyes.

2. Sit for meditation. Close your eyes and meditate for ten minutes. Without opening your eyes or losing the meditation trance, begin to play the djembe. Continue for ten minutes.

3. Make a circle of friends. Add some meditation. Add some beats. Then add some dance. Close your eyes. Take off the masks. Find the truth. Continue for a long, long time. Occasionally, add a new friend. Is the resulting circle like any other circle?

4. Plan someone's birthday party as a magical or ritual celebration. That is, you must clearly define what is banished, what is invoked, what the circle is, and where the taboos are. Are there talismans you can make? Are there ecstatic trance elements you can create or use? What is the difference between such a "magical'" birthday party and an "ordinary" birthday party?

Questions

1. What is the practical limit of a circle? Discuss the occult meaning of a circle. What are the limits of the form of a circle? How does the form of a circle affect the wyrd?
2. What makes a circle scary as you approach its limit?
3. What is the difference between the taboo of images in subtle perception and the perception of power?
4. Discuss power, taboo, and wyrd as applied to circles.
5. Discuss the attempted murder of Dionysus and why you can't kill the triple-born god.
6. What is the wyrd of ecstasy?
7. What are the taboos of ecstasy? Discuss taboo in terms of a trance party.
8. At a party, how much of the decoration adds to the wyrd? In what ways can decoration or costuming become taboo and add to the wyrd of a trance party?
9. What does the music add? In which ways can music be taboo? Is ultrasonic music taboo?
10. Discuss how attitude adds to or takes away from the wyrd of the party?
11. Discuss the wyrd effects of a party from an individual as well as global perspectives.
12. Discuss the effects of alcohol or drug addiction on ecstatic trance in terms of the wyrd and taboos.

Magic

What is magic?

Magic is the process of transformation or a modification of destiny by the skillful use of the wyrd; in other words, it is the art of making things happen.

What follows here may seem like an overly technical explanation of something fundamentally simple. Magic can be expressed by other terms and perspectives and has been. "Believe and it shall be" is one simple alternative way to express the principle of magic. "Repeat and visualize" is another. Franz Bardon,[64] Johannes Trithemius,[65] the Ikhwan al-Safa,[66] and many others developed and elaborated complex rituals and symbols for "doing magic," but the simple principles which underlie all forms of magic are: repetition, trance, and visualization.

Reality is fundamentally malleable because of the basic interconnectedness of everything, but this perspective is not usually believed nor understood how it could be so. There is an extremely powerful almost universal trance that hides or covers this basic interconnectedness, the universal consciousness, so that the illusion most people believe is that we are all separate. Access to the universal consciousness seems to be taboo. We can't go there

---

[64] Franz Bardon (1910-1958) was one of the most remarkable magicians of the twentieth century.
[65] Johannes Trithemius (1462-1516) one of the central figures in the evolution of the Western Esoteric Tradition.
[66] A Hermetic brotherhood of the tenth and eleventh centuries whose encyclopedia the Rasa'il influenced the Picatrix: Ghayat al-Hakim (Goal of the Wise) an important connection between Hermetic philosophy and the esoteric traditions of the Middle East.

from here unless we fundamentally change ourselves. People also tend to believe that there must be an intercession between our entranced selves and universal consciousness. They believe that agent of intercession is the priest, shaman, or magician. The hermetic approach is that the alchemist must change or purify himself before the symbolic lead can be transmuted into the symbolic gold. Presumably, the priest, shaman, magician, and alchemist all have purified themselves by austerities including meditation for many years. In so doing they have broken through the great illusion, the taboo. They then arrive to a position in which they can do magic and intercede when others suffer.

Let us examine what magic is from the perspective of a young magician, as an example. The first big problem for a magician is to fully understand the universal trance, to break through the taboo of knowing who you really are. Breaking this taboo needs a lot of personal courage. It means doing a lot of self introspection, discovering and owning your own personal power and responsibility, and discovering and following the inner truth that leads to universal consciousness. The main tool a magician has is meditation, a trance that uncovers the most subtle and increases the skillful means of the wyrd.

Used skillfully by means of trance the wyrd also modifies and transforms the magician, perceptions, cognitive functions, and the means of action, and consequently the wyrd can transform reality itself by any measure. A false step in this process results in delusion and madness.

Trance, the ancient way of personal transformation, is alchemical in the sense that you are both the object and subject of a sacred experiment; it all begins and ends with you; and the work itself is repetitive and continuous. Realizing this fundamental process is the sacred work that a witch, priest, yogi, alchemist, or magician is intending to do by developing their magical skills.

There is often a perception of magic as indistinguishable from the wyrd energies it uses. If the wyrd is strong, then there is magic; if there is no wyrd, there is no magic and everything is normal.

This definition of magic as the skillful use of wyrd energy is equally a useful definition for stage magic, illusion, slight of hand, and other forms of deception, since effective deception also requires the presence of some wyrd energy. The primary difference between weak magic, like stage magic, and powerful real magic, like the actions of the gods, is the difference in the strength or intensity of the wyrd. Trance is generally a way or technique of increasing, modifying, or controlling the wyrd energy. That is, to effectively use and control trance is also to control magical energy.

The reality of a glass of water can be described as being sustained by a wyrd of high energy and appearing as a separate object. In addition, because it is taboo to realize universal consciousness, one normally cannot see or understand what creates the glass of water. It is a "secret" or a "mystery." Meditation, hypnosis, and addictive trance can modify the apparent reality of the glass of water to an unlimited degree. Such trances can make a glass of water disappear to oneself and everyone around. Or the water can turn into wine. Or the glass of water can turn into vibuti. What do you understand as a glass of water?

One of the reasons there is so much mystery about magic is that so few people can really effectively control the wyrd. Magicians and spiritual people recommend meditation as one of the best ways to gain important skills in controlling the wyrd—although they don't express it in that way. Scientists are very effective in controlling the wyrd through technology; this control comes from long hours of technical concentration on various scientific principles—doubtless a form of meditation in which taboos are broken and subtle universal truths are discovered. Medical miracles are thereby produced. Some technical nerds can also develop special magical skills due to long focused hours in a technical trance. Your computer can be fixed or destroyed by such technical nerds. Artists too can change reality by altering themselves and the wyrd with the consequence that a play, a painting, a piece of music, etc., can transform the consumer of such creations.

And what about those who do not know how to, can not, or do not control the wyrd in any way and are subject to the wyrd of these magicians? They might become innocent or fearful victims to the extent that they are in awe of their magic. Awe is, after all, a kind of wyrd. With knowledge, every potential and actual victim can begin their own transformation. Victims can also become alchemists or magicians. But first they must become aware of various magical principles.

By explaining that it is the control of the trance wyrd that is responsible for effectiveness in changing destiny, I am not claiming that any particular group has more or less skill than any other group. Some Catholic monks, due to long hours of prayer and meditation, have developed effective magical skills equal to or better than many highly qualified research scientists. At the same time, I must add that some folks, due to the trauma of war, prison, illness, grief, or family psychology, have learned magic through habits of repetitive fixation on various abstract ideas, which induce trance and allows them to overcome all sorts of personal pain and dysfunction. They may, after some time, emerge with highly developed healing or psychic skills. So, each and all of these groups share, in common, the experience of repeating something mentally for a long time and in so doing arrive at some point in their lives with real magical skills—the ability to effectively transform one reality to another.

Transformation and Destiny

Transformation is a change in the way consciousness behaves or processes. When the cohesiveness of association is high, then there is no change in the mental processing or behavior and one's destiny can be predicted.

The wyrd modifies the cohesiveness and therefore allows consciousness to change. The wyrd is associated with magic and therefore the wyrd is responsible for a change in destiny and consciousness. So, if we can gain some conscious control over the wyrd, we can begin to do magic. In so doing, we will also change ourselves and modify our own destiny. We must be without fear and have courage to do this. Eliminating fear first of all requires knowledge.

The wyrd begins to manifest earliest as simple dissociation. This is the baby wyrd and it is not very strong, so it does not usually produce much transformation or change in destiny. Yet, it could easily give rise to a new idea of what to have for dinner; it can be the basis for learning new ideas. Daydreams and nightmares in a certain way fit into this level. The really long-term sustained but controlled dissociations start to get more interesting. One starts to break through the ordinary realms of association and conscious-ness, and a free rein is given to explore new possibilities without the hindrances or barriers. Within this long-term sustained and controlled dissociation—brought about by meditation or other ways—certain subtleties begin to reveal themselves. Some new connections begin to be made. Of course, when you just start, it may be difficult to maintain the trance for any length of time, but there are ways to sustain it; merely add or start additional trances and maintain them for long periods of time.

Action of the Wyrd

Fundamentally, the wyrd is the energy created by a trance, but it is also a reflection of the energy needed to break a trance. When a trance is constantly present, the wyrd becomes like a field or standing wave of energy, which influences or alters the local area. Whenever a strong trance is maintained for a long period of time, the wyrd will begin to warp or pull the local reality into coherence with it. If you are creating a new reality and you sustain the wyrd—while in a trance—a twisting or torsion is produced as the old reality transforms into the new reality. This is subjectively experienced by everyone in the local area as a kind of strong, strange weirdness (wyrd) or some kind of spooky energy. Some people have visual sensations such as going through some kind of door, or the visual fabric seems to fall away as in a psychedelic experience. Some Tibetan lamas generate strong wyrds during rituals. During the Tibetan Black Crown

Ceremony, in which the Karmapa manifests Avalokateshvara, a strong wyrd is generated and subjectively experienced by the spectators. Some people actually see the Karmapa change into another being. Satya Sai Baba also generates a strong wyrd force when he manifests vibuti. In fields of war, where focused minds both defend themselves, kill others, and are themselves killed, the wyrd is palpable.

The mere presence of the wyrd does not mean that it is precisely controlled. As I mentioned above, the wyrd can be generated by intense fear and a focused mind. Precise control of the wyrd comes more from long years of meditation practice or sometimes by trauma. The wyrd can also be created by electronic invasive trance induction techniques as well as drugs, but such magic is not victimless.

Ritual

Which bring us to ritual magic.67 Ritual is a form of taboo used to increase the wyrd. I am using the word taboo here in a special and technical sense. Taboo physically expresses the idea of dissociation. It does not require intercession, but naturally requires skillful means. If you are not skillful in the means, then you better stay away from the power. You can also use the word taboo to mean that you don't mess with the innards of your cell phone unless you have the skillful means to do so. If you violate the taboo, you will probably break the magic too. By respecting the taboo, you enable the power. Going into a hospital operating room "unpurified" is also taboo. Ritual magic has similar requirements as a taboo.

Some kinds of misunderstanding have developed regarding magic and ritual that has resulted in the destruction of the wyrd.

A long time ago there was the idea that ritual-ecstasy-celebration maintained over a period of time could have an influence on the weather, on crops, on illness, and so on. Somehow,

---

[67] Electronic invasive trance induction techniques are also a form of ritual (black) magic. Ritual magic also has victims.

perhaps the ego got involved, the ridiculous idea developed that if a magician were really good and the magic that was produced were really strong, then results would be fairly instant. Since all competing magicians want to be the strongest magicians, the rituals may have gotten shorter and shorter with belief, dogma, and delusion becoming the more important components of ritual and the progressive development of the wyrd became less important. The general commercialization and compartmenting of activity and intent has further weakened the wyrd by scattering energy. If you don't have time to meditate, it will be impossible to develop strong wyrds, no matter how much money you have for magical trinkets. If the wyrd is not strong, any ritual mainly becomes empty delusion and superstition.

Ritual magic is the external manifestation of the inner. First, you meditate and develop the inner awareness. You add hypnotic components and the wyrd becomes stronger. You add addictive/devotional types of trances by including ritual or elements of this world into the trance. At some point, the wyrd becomes very strong and palpable to others, but it is not compelling until you develop the charismatic trance structure. Whenever a charismatic trance contains disrupting chaotic[68] and reforming ecstatic[69] energy, your magic creates a compulsive potential in the local causal area. That is, when a charismatic trance is used, the ritual appears to alter the local reality.

If you are a shaman, alchemist, priest, Wiccan, magician, or yogi, you may have noticed that celebratory rituals become more effective if you first invest your time in building the foundation of a meditation trance. Then you can subsequently build on the meditation trance in a consistent manner, by first adding hypnotic forms, then addictive, and finally charismatic forms, including ritual (taboo) and ecstasy. If you examine many traditional rituals, you can discover abbreviated examples of this formula, likewise with abbreviated results. Such abbreviated

---

[68] Chaos breaks prior forms.
[69] Multiple trances provide a stochastic wave statistically in favor of a desirable outcome.

ritual results in a kind of entertainment, fascination, or intoxication sufficient for many purposes.

Magic can seem like a form of intoxication to others, but it is also an important part of the inner-external nature of the addictive/devotional/ecstatic trance form. To many people, this aspect is very scary because reality really does start to alter. As the wyrd grows over time, the charismatic/numinous forms of trance start to manifest when others become automatically swept into the trance. Some shamans and yogis—at least those who are authentic enough to spend hours really meditating—will have developed strong enough wyrds that the local reality tangibly alters. As mentioned earlier, the Black Crown Ceremony of the Karmapa, in which Avalokateshvara is actually manifested, is an example of a strong wyrd altering the local reality.

At that point, the ritual/ecstatic external form technically becomes a numinous trance. The numinous form is when the fence between the One and the Two breaks down and the Original Love manifests. Death manifests also as part of the banishment; life and death become one. I think this magic is what shamans, priests, Wiccans, yogis, and Popes are actually aiming for, but for many reasons explained above is very difficult to achieve. One must have a crazy determination to face the fear of death of your reality.

Purpose

Why do magic? Even if you don't get as far as being able to manifest Original Love, there are many of benefits for the would-be magician.

The solitary yogi or witch can benefit personally and socially by taking the first step along the way: long meditation is an excellent preparation for ritual magic.

When the hypnotic form of trance is added to a regimen of meditation, the wyrd begins to get stronger. Objects used in these forms can become magically charged to a certain extent.

What is also vital is to maintain and repeat the object of your magic. Moreover, the object of the magic must be found in every subtle manifestation. This is really the work of the alchemist, to extract the gold from the lead through purification and transformation, to bring what is not there into existence. This is an old precept. Marcilio Ficino, a fifteenth century alchemist, wrote:

"If you want your body and spirit to receive power from the Sun, learn which are the Solar things among metals and stones, even more among plants, but among the animal world most of all . . . To invoke the sun's power, you put on Solar things to wear, you live in Solar places, look Solar, hear Solar, smell Solar, imagine Solar, think Solar, and even desire Solar."

Expressed in this way, you might begin to understand that ritual magic cannot be just a hobby; it is a full-time job.

When ritual is added to the meditative and hypnotic forms of trance, one could say that Will becomes involved. This is what Crowley was writing about. Some of the old Christian monks could become so devoted in their addictive/devotional trances that they could endure many austerities and personal sacrifices. Yet, this addictive/devotional trance form is still but a single step on the way. Siddhis develop easily in the addictive/devotional trance forms. Siddhis can make one wildly happy, and as the wyrd becomes stronger, this general happiness and excitement can spread to the local community. Parties happen. Celebration and ecstasy seems just the natural thing to do.

At some point, the celebration and ritual/ecstasy and wild happiness seems to become an epidemic locally. The wyrd becomes very strong and magic seems to be everywhere, but no one seems to be doing anything obvious. Yet, the inner Being is being manifested. The differences between people dissolve as everyone is compelled to see the commonality of the shared reality. This is the Two becoming One, and Love is expressed. This could be the ancient meaning of agape.

Structure

To make magic happen, there must be a structure that provides the limits and focuses the wyrd. It is an arbitrary structure, but most magicians use a circle. An altar is also a limiting structure that works. A cathedral or a cave is also an example of a limiting structure. So is a grave. The shamans of the Pacific islands would wrap their talismanic gods in bark in order to increase and control the power of these magical icons. So, the idea of a limit or taboo in order to focus the wyrd is really quite an old one. Taboo in the west is not a common idea. Taboo is most often associated with superstition, but I am using taboo in a different, more general and technical sense here to indicate a kind of covering to limit and focus the wyrd. When the taboo is made physically manifest, it becomes a talisman.

Generally, to increase power the wyrd must be bound or covered by a taboo. In some cases this is nothing more than a circle. It can also be secrecy. It can be any kind of limit that separates the self from the other, the holy from the profane. When the taboo is missing, the wyrd is considerably dispersed.

It would seem that a trance party would also need a limit or a larger circle for the wyrd to become concentrated. A string, a line of salt, a wisp of incense smoke circumscribing the party would also work.

And although a rectangular altar is topologically the same as a circle, the straight line edge of the altar probably weakens the wyrd.

Evaluation of Effects and Causes

How can one ever know if magic works? If magic is truly effective, it changes both the experience as well as the one experiencing. The independent observer is changed; any scientific instrumentation is also changed. Because any transformation also changes the magician, it is impossible to "own" the effect of magic, that is, to say that the magician caused the effect. Also, effective magic creates the Other—that's the point, after all—so, in some strange sense, when "nothing happens" the magic has been effective.

Exercises

1. In your next magical circle, calculate the wyrd by counting how many times an act is repeated. How long is the ritual? Are the trance structures meditation, hypnotic, addictive, charismatic, ecstatic? Are the trances additive or sequential?
2. Next time you see something scary or chaotic happening, identify the trance and estimate the wyrd. Locate the taboo, if you can.

Questions

1. Discuss the Tablets of Moses and a few of the magical practices of Agrippa from the perspectives you learn in this chapter.
2. Find three places or situations in which you find effective magic. Analyze and justify your reasons for thinking so.
3. Find three places or situations in which magic is proclaimed to exist, but it is not effective. Analyze, justify, and describe why using the ideas of the trance model might help to increase the wyrd.
4. The circle is pagan and the line is roman. What is the function of salt in terms of trance theory?
5. What is essential to oracular magic?
6. Find ten examples of ritual in modern life and identify the taboo, the talisman, the wyrd, the victims, and the trance. Start with television.

Advanced Trance

IF TRANCE IS SUBTLE, ADVANCED TRANCE is even more subtle. The main objective of advanced trance is the development of a finer, more detailed transcendent experience: to research the parameters in detail that lead to the creation of an efficient trance, including the building of taboos and talismans, and to increase, sustain, and direct or focus the trance wyrd. Avoiding the inadvertent creation of trance-related problems is another goal. Due to certain risks associated with trance, developing, understanding, and applying some trance safety engineering techniques is also prudent.

Developing finer subtle perception requires much practical experience starting with meditation and hypnosis. There are many traditional ways to develop and enhance subtle perception. One traditional way is through yoga. Another way is by personal experimentation with meditation, hypnotic trance, and addictive trance structures. Lucid dream and sleep techniques are also very helpful. Chemically, biologically, or electronically induced trance may be helpful if done wisely, prudently, and in homeopathic doses. Enhancing the wyrd by discovering new or using already known techniques for creating taboos and talismans is also helpful as well.

If you follow a guru or one of the traditional avenues of trance development, you will soon discover that almost without exception experimentation with trance is firmly discouraged. There are many good reasons for this. Trance disables good judgment and memory, so uncontrolled experimentation with trance will likely result in a world of confusion, upset, and delusion. The history of the world contains many insane madmen, and psychotic lost souls, who are the products of trance experimentation gone awry. There is a solution to this problem: good trance engineering. This means take experimental risks only in small steps and only go into unknown areas from which you can easily get out. One way to do this is to consciously mark—maybe even write down—or notice a clear inventory of your cognitive functions before setting out to experiment. Do not pile up one trance experiment on top of another. Wait until you get to a prior known consciousness and fully recover from your experiment. Make certain that any of your newly created trances are fully terminated before starting a new one. This is easier said than done. There is often a high that comes from unterminated trance, and it is very easy to become seduced into delusional states. It can really be exhilarating to discover new powers of the mind, and you might be so excited you might want to try piling on more. The wise way is to terminate the trance, even though you like it. That way you develop control.

One experiment you can do, is to start a meditation trance and after twenty minutes of using your regular mantra, change the mantra to "little furry creatures" for another twenty minutes, and then get up without terminating the trance. Within the next few hours, notice if you see anything different, especially out of the corners of your eyes. Also notice how long this "tranceling effect" persists. Hours? Days? Weeks? You will get an idea of the potential danger unterminated trances can bring. Terminate the "little furry creature" trance by doing your regular grounding meditation and thus reestablishing your former consciousness. Then end your meditation firmly. That is, in fact, the way to terminate every trance experiment: reestablish your former consciousness. And the safety rule is: don't go so far out with any one trance that you forget your way back or can't get back to whatever "normal" is for you.

To be absolutely safe and successful, your advanced trance experiments must be carefully monitored by a qualified third party both for safety and for technical reasons. If your monitor says you are losing your memory or not using good sense, take them seriously and start hunting your own trancelings. There is nothing as personally bothersome as an out-of-control trance.

The primary danger is that trancelings can make you become forgetful, or selectively blind, create visuals that don't exist, or create false memories and false beliefs (delusions). The main reason for having a monitor is that you have a second set of eyes focused on you to make sure that when you terminate your trances, they are all terminated. A monitor or third party is not a guru or priest. You don't need religious advice or suggestions when you need to hunt trancelings.

Balance of the mind is an important key to clarity, health, and success in trance. Although absolute balance may be impossible in this world, perhaps conditions may be created so that balance can be maintained for a short duration. In such a period of balance the techniques of advanced trance can be more successful.

Advanced trance all happens within the mind, so whatever helps mental balance, in general, also helps create favorable conditions for advanced trance practices.

Some common and traditional indicators of mental imbalance are: greed, ignorance, anger, jealousy, pride, and obsession. Although this list looks very much like a medieval list of sins, it still is a good guideline for evaluating your mental balance. While it is possible to practice trance angry and greedy, you should use trance, in that case, only to regain your balance. The subtle areas of advanced trance are not available to an unbalanced mind any more than you can compete successfully in a sport when you are not in top condition or, for example, jealous. In such a case, you risk hurting yourself or others. In the case of trance, you risk your own sanity. This is important to remember.

The object of discussing advanced trance is to indicate a subtle relationship between cause and effect. As we discussed in earlier chapters, the effects of trance modify perception and the wyrd. Because of these modifications, meaning in a trance can be very different outside of a trance. Perhaps this is one reason ancient texts describing the causes and effects of trance become abstract, symbolic, allegorical, and mystical. Moreover, the altered perceptions of each person in a trance is different, despite having identical causes or use of the same trance techniques.

An ancient Tibetan text may describe a meditation technique with definite and explicit symbols, mantras, mandalas, visualization, colors, and so on. And under perfect conditions and environment the same practice done anywhere should have the same effects. But conditions have changed in the world in ways unforeseen by the ancients. For example, chemical, electronic, magnetic pollution, as well as other wyrd energies are now part of the environment and vary from place to place. While the ancient techniques may still be effective, the changed conditions of this Yuga[70] require careful circumspection before embarking on an ancient practice.

Specifically, anyone trying to practice advanced trance must be fully aware that there are two kinds of causes of trance: There are the causes you have control over and there are causes you do not have control over. This means that there are general background trances going on, and there are trance effects that you yourself create. Being as aware as possible in order to distinguish these two kinds of causes and effects is critical to success in advanced trance. In addition, it is important to be aware that trance modifies perception, so a background trance effect very likely will appear different from the internal trance perspective. In some ways this can be a benefit: some nasty externally caused trances may seem benign from a normal perception, but expose their malignancy when perceived from a trance. Healers, for example, can recognize cancers and other non-obvious health problems by means of the altered perception they achieve while in a trance. On the other hand, general background "enchantments" can make invisible conditions that could be obvious otherwise.

It is the unique combinations of disabled cognitive functions and of the order in which they are created, that produces all of the strange and wild occult states. By this I mean that if you start

---

[70]The Kali Yuga.

a trance generating loop and because of this first loop you go into unconscious sleep, you can just forget about going on your shamanic journey. If you want to go on a shamanic journey, you must only start trance generating loops under conditions where losing complete consciousness is not an option.

Most "fancy" occult trance states—such as siddhis—are built up over a somewhat long period of time. In this progressive learning process, first, one type of cognitive function is disabled and controlled, then perhaps another one. Then some subtle cognitive functions are enhanced or amplified by suggestion or by further controlling any distractions. Slowly, these trances are allowed to stabilize almost like letting a wine age. That is, you learn precise control. They must also be broken periodically, so that one does not lose the sense of ordinary reality and also to be able to test the strength of the wyrd.

Occult altered states are not simple to produce consistently, because each person is different. A simple trance for one person might disable a targeted cognitive function, but for another person the same trance disables the wrong cognitive function. Creating trances in a haphazard or careless way can create weird altered states, which look to others very much like mental pathologies. It is possible to create addictive dissociated states that are not pleasant, such as paranoia, delusions, persistent nightmares, and so on. It is for this reason that one must test that the desired effects are produced by a trance and that there are no undesirable effects. If you are desperate to produce some sort of occult state, reconsider. The dangers are great. Randomly created trances usually create delusion and expose you to pathological trances. Many trances produced in this way are dangerous, because you can get psychically lost in them. This is because multiple trances can become fixed—relatively permanent—and one stays more or less permanently in an addictive trance. Goodbye, life.

The use of images, idols, symbols, mandalas, and generally talismans of all sorts has been a tradition of yogis and magicians, etc. for millennia. They are often combined with taboo.

Fundamentally, they all used talismans deliberately as part of an hypnotic trance loop to increase the wyrd for magic ritual, for initiations, for teaching, or as an aid to inner visualization.

For mandalas combined with contemplation or meditation—whether Tibetan or Sufi—a similar analysis applies. Repetition creates a dissociated trance plane and consequent disabling of some cognitive functions. This would also be a hypnotic trance since part of the loop is "outside." It is only when the entire loop is "inside" that it is a meditation trance. Some mandalas are used as teaching mechanisms. During the teaching process, the type of trance is hypnotic. After the student knows what the mandala looks like, it can be visualized internally. Once the internal visualization is robust, the hypnotic trance becomes a meditation trance. What is interesting is that there are then two mandalas: an inner one and an external one. As the inner mandala is explored and made more vivid and subtle aspects are discovered and experienced, the external mandala acquires a taboo. That is, the inner mandala creates a secret aspect of the external mandala, or one could say the external mandala hides or covers additional meanings discoverable only through meditation.

Developing Your Trance Skills

Trance as an ability to multiprocess can—with practice—become a valuable skill. It is quite important to be able to go into a trance, stop a trance, and to allocate cognitive skills to tasks both consciously as well as consciously. It is not necessary to have a hypnotist do this.

Terminating a simple trance usually is successful by interrupting the primary trance generating loop. Deep and complex (not simple) trances usually have secondary loops and that is what makes them more stable. Often, breaking the secondary loop does no good because it is quickly reestablished. Another way is to interrupt the secondary loop and insert suggestions to break the primary loop. Nonsense words can be used also. But one must be aware as to the effect the nonsense words have on the dissociated plane. Nonsense words can also drive one deeper into a trance.

Unwanted moods and states means you have missed something. Probably if you meditate it would occur to you and then the mood would change. Meditation is a trance. The trance disables a cognitive function—like judgment—long enough to allow the missed something to be found. This results in the mood being changed in some way.

As to strong trance forces, I agree that a desire to create them may arise from pathological need. What may be more efficient in the long run is to have some skill with trance in general rather than focus merely on maximizing a force. I suspect that focusing solely on maximizing the trance force will cause damage to the ego structure—in other words, one might go crazy. And I am sure people have. On the other hand, the skillful use of trance can really do magic by the purposeful and precise use of the wyrd.

It is just as difficult for me to explain in a simple way how to build a strong trance force as it would be for me to explain in a simple way how to be a violin virtuoso. But I guess "practice, practice, practice" is not a bad way to start. For all the Trance Theory detail and discussion, there is no simple, easy "just-add-two-eggs and stir" or "chant the magic mantra" way to do it.

Meditation is, however, a good way to start. Regular, long-term practice works the best. Meditation creates a simple trance, so meditating gives one a lot of inner experience when done over a period of years. Along with this, I would suggest the use of hypnotic techniques, including ritual magic, or the use of external and symbolic loops, circles. The external appearance of things is not as important as the inner awareness created. Shifting awareness from one trance to another, traversing the ego along the nodes of a structure makes sense when the skill level and inner awareness are developed sufficiently to allow this. Developing trance in the context of lucid dreaming is very helpful.

Here is a table that distinguishes between the skillful use of trance and what we might find when trance is not skillfully done:

Skillful use of trance	Unskillful
abstraction	learning difficulties
Use of symbols	confuse symbol with thing
Meditation	belief bound fantasies
Creative	Dull, literal
Hypnotic, persuasive	Follows orders uncritically
Magical powers	Multiple addictions
Enlightenment	Ordinary, non-creative
Deathless	inert, slothful, greedy

Developing Meditation Skills

Meditation, when practiced regularly and consistently, will prove to be a valuable aid toward the learning and development of many trance skills.

When skills are developed in trance, which is to say, when a person can easily invoke a trance and yet retain some control over the trance, then he or she may be ready for the adventure of Advanced Trance work.

When a trance is created and sustained, trance wyrds are also created and may be felt. With time and effort it is possible to learn to control the trance wyrds.

If you want to develop some Advanced Trance skills, then use the following as a guide:

1. First, eliminate as far as possible, other trances. Prior hypnotic and addictive trances create trance wyrds, which interfere with the creation of your own self-induced trance wyrd. Therefore, if you wish to develop your own trance wyrd, it is critical to eliminate all those "alien" trances, those which you have not created.

All addictive and charismatic trances should be eliminated, so far as possible. I know this is not an easy task.

2. Secondly, practice some form of meditation, in order to establish and develop your own trance wyrd. It is important to practice consistently over a long period of time. It is not desirable to practice meditation for more than three hours per day in the beginning. But, after a few years of daily meditation practice, practicing for three or four hours per day would be beneficial.

The purpose of meditation is to develop independence from thoughts and to gain the skills to both create and destroy your personal trances at will.

Thoughts can be disturbing. Day-to-day events, as well as traumatic past events, can be a source of worry, depression, or hyperactivity, which can be self-destructive. These disturbing thoughts consume energy as well. We need to use all available energy to create a strong trance wyrd. Therefore, it is necessary to eliminate disturbing thoughts. One way to do this is to meditate, in order to establish independence from your thoughts.

At the same time, it is also necessary to become free, so far as possible, from the attraction or repulsion of specific thoughts and ideas. Meditation will allow all sorts of ideas and thoughts to appear. Some will be beautiful and some will be horrible. The experience of these thoughts will be in the dissociated trance plane. You must endeavor to disable your censor or that critical part of your mind that passes judgments on thoughts. Allow them all. Their free energy will increase the trance wyrd. If you must spend energy repressing your thoughts, then you will lose some of your ability to create strong trance wyrds.

3. Thirdly, be certain that the primary meditation trance you create does not contain hypnotic suggestions. The thought objects in the primary trance generating loop should be neutral, so far as possible.

Religious based meditations or meditations that contain specific hypnotic suggestions or delusional beliefs are not very useful for producing the maximum trance wyrd. One must be quite careful in choosing the "mantra" so that it does not contain such undesirable specific hypnotic content.

To be quite clear: your first or primary meditation trance should not be based on a specific false hypnotic suggestion or a specific delusion.

4. Fourth, establish secondary trance generating loops you can control. If you cannot control these secondary loops, then you run the danger of becoming addicted or seriously mentally ill. Giving up control to a guru, priest, hypnotist, or popular cult leader is not a good idea either. Unfortunately, mediated trance situations do not produce the controls you need; you can't subcontract meditation or get it from a church, a drug dealer, or buy it at the store. Unlike the secondary loops of an addict or schizophrenic, these secondary order trance generating loops should not have content and they should have neither desirable nor undesirable side effects. If they have desirable or undesirable side effects, then the trances will probably become hypnotic first and then addictive. The purpose of the secondary trance generating loops is to increase the trance wyrd and nothing more.

When secondary trance generating loops have desirable side effects, they will very likely become addictive. When a television commercial convinces you to buy something that you decide you like and find useful, you will naturally tend to like television and find it useful. This kind of secondary loop is at the basis of an addiction to television. This is the fundamental reason that it is important that the secondary loops have no desirable side effects. They should be neutral.

The following is true for every ordinary trance: A trance is created; it is sustained for some time, and then it terminates or collapses. After it collapses, there is a reconstruction-collapse (r-c) cycle similar to an echo or an after wave.

Because a trance is created from a trance generating loop, the analysis of trance as a wave phenomenon is suggested as a research project. The reconstruction-collapse phenomenon, which happens after the trance terminates, seems related to some "magical" phenomena that subsequently occurs. The reconstruction-collapse cycle does not necessarily happen immediately after the termination of a trance. The reason for this is unclear.

The primary difference between an ordinary trance and an Advanced Trance is that there is much more control and sensitivity in the creation, sustaining, and collapse of the Advanced Trance. During the sustaining phase, there may be interaction with other trances—creating something like interference patterns—and this allows the cognitive functions to be "tuned." But obviously you can't "tune" anything if you are not aware of the interference patterns and only experience them.

Here is a simple example:

Lie back and listen to a Bach cantata or some reggae or jazz—and watch or pay attention to how each musical loop creates a trance, and how that trance interacts with other trances (from other musical loops) before it collapses. You have to practice and be in a fairly calm, relaxed state of mind without too much noise, otherwise you might not notice the creation and collapse of a trance, because it is very subtle. It is somewhat easier to notice with shamanic drumming or an Indian raga, since the loops are few, regular, and sustained. The typical trance-dance musical loops are often too numerous, irregular, and not sustained enough to work as examples.

Once you have done this and you notice the interference patterns created by a collapsing trance, then do the same thing with meditation, and then with hypnosis. Then repeat with both meditation and hypnosis. Are you beginning to understand the subtlety and power of trance?

Intermediate Advanced Trance

I will now briefly discuss the more serious, non-secular intermediate advance trance. For this discussion, our perspective is that from devotional trance and charismatic trance forms.

In these forms of trance, the ego function is detached from normal secular channels and attention is on the most subtle of inner senses. This also transforms the ego from that which goes out to that which goes in. In this sense, the ego becomes sacrificial, humble, open without an I/ego.

The objects of action also are transformed. The hand does not move the chalice, but the inner hand moves the chalice. The objects of inner sense become more acute; records and information available on the inner realities become readable and intelligible.

At first, like a child, action is not so skilled, perception is not fully integrated with knowledge, and the experiences are not clear, nor persistent. So, they seem like a dream, and the dream is what we normally experience when we dream. But, with practice of trance, the dream becomes clear. The secular ego is abandoned for the more permanent, clear "divine" ego. Once the secular ego is abandoned, the inner worlds become real and the secular world becomes the dream. This is a real state of the inner child devotional trance. So, the inner child can read, but not really understand these records and intelligences. Celebration and love on the inner is too much for the child, and the inner child must go to bed while the adults have their scene. The inner child makes up stories and fantasies as to what the inner divine adult must be doing.

When the inner divine child grows up and has more inner experience, the inner divine adult experiences celebrations and love, similar to celebration and love one finds in the secular world as charisma.

Finding Your Own Way

IF TRANCE WILL HAVE ANY MEANING at all in your life, then you must become even more aware of it. If not, then you can quickly become a pawn, a victim of those who will use trance against you in order to exploit your unconsciousness.

There are many opportunities to learn more about trance. Of course, one practical way is to practice meditation and learn by direct experience about the deep nature of your own mind.

At some point in the practice of meditation you may wish to expand your experiences with experimentation. Meditation trance, over time, naturally exposes you to the potential for adding hypnotic, addictive, and charismatic trances.

Finding others with whom you can share your internal experiences at some point becomes very valuable. Exploring trance by yourself can be a lonely undertaking replete with dangers of all kinds. Having associates with more or less the same kind of experiences is assuring and provides some degree of safety when exploring new trance forms.

Expressing your internal realizations in the form of actualizations is a natural consequence of deep trance work. Some people become interested in the subtle nature of plants and use that knowledge to extend their experiential reach. Others are more social and explore the possibilities of reaching others. By using trance, your natural skills may develop in interesting ways expressing your universal potential more fully.

This world is changing. Understanding the universal nature of consciousness within a world of changes needs practical experience and this is most efficiently realized through the individual practice of trance in its many forms.

Dennis R. Wier

As chaos manifests again and again, destroying everything, the most potent seeds for the future can be found within the development of your personal universal consciousness today.

Glossary

addictive trance: A type of triple loop trance characterized by a primary inner (meditation) trance generating loop (TGL) and a secondary hypnotic trance loop, which has some elements in the primary dissociated trance plane, and a third loop, which characterizes the repetitive compulsive behavior of the addiction. The primary inner trance is usually taboo—hidden from the addict—adding to the power (wyrd) of the trance. See also devotion.

charismatic trance: A type of quadruple loop trance characterized by an addictive trance with the addition of a fourth loop that creates compulsive co-dependent behaviors in others.

cognitive function: A mental ability or thinking process.

cognitive loop: A repeating sequence of cognitive objects.

cognitive object: Any thought, feeling, or inner sensation.

cohesiveness of association: A measure of the associative richness, depth or complexity of a cognitive object.

complex trance: A trance with multiple trance generating loops that create mixtures of meditation, hypnotic, and addictive trance forms.

critical judgment: The ability to correctly reason from causes.

destiny: The results of the actions of a system of cognitive functions.

domain: The set of cognitive objects used by a cognitive function for a specific mental process. See also range.

devotion: Another term for an addictive trance. A devotional trance has the same structural form as an addictive trance, but a devotional trance is controllable and the inner meditation trance is not taboo.

dissociated trance plane (DTP): The specific set of modified cognitive functions that result from a trance.

dissociation: A subjectively perceived cognitive condition in which conscious self awareness seems set apart from other conscious self awareness processes.

hypnotic trance: A trance created by two trance generating loops. One results in a primary meditation trance. Some of the second trance generating loop comes from a source (the hypnotist) external to the subject and some of it comes from within the meditation trance. The primary meditation trance is taboo.

loop running time: The time that it takes to repeat one loop of cognitive objects.

meditation trance: A trance created by the repetition of a single trance generating loop in which the entire loop is internal or consisting entirely of cognitive objects.

mutual trance: A hypnotic trance in which the primary trance generating loop is shared by two individuals.

pathological trance: A fundamentally unhealthy trance that unfavorably restricts choice, disallows personal responsibility, and results in an impoverished condition.

primary induction: The process or act of starting any trance generating loop on which further trances will be constructed.

range: The set of possible cognitive objects that may result from the operation of a specific cognitive function. See also domain.

secondary trance loop: Any associating additional cognitive loop between a dissociated trance plane and its primary trance generating loop. The purpose of secondary trance loops is to stabilize the primary trance by creating another trance.

taboo: 1. The conscious self, active within a trance, who generates a wyrd which is protected or focused by a distinguishing cover. 2. As perceived by others, an object, being the covered wyrd of a trance.

talisman: 1. A venerated object, thought to contain the magical, frightening, and powerful energies of an unknown mysterious source. 2. A taboo made into a physical object by covering, protecting, or making secret any trance that generates a strong wyrd.

thought object: See cognitive object.

time to trance: The duration from the commencement of a trance generating loop until there is a trance.

trance: 1. A specific type of dissociation created by the repetition of cognitive objects and resulting in one or more disabled cognitive functions. 2. To go into a trance or to put into a trance; to entrance.

trance abuse: Any deliberate exploitation of a person (victim) who is in a trance without prior informed consent.

trance collapse: The event and effects of the termination of the dissociated trance plane. Sometimes this is experienced as a kind of shock as some cognitive functions stop and others are re-enabled. The shock is a measurable neuro-physiological effect of the wyrd.

trance delta: The elapsed time between the start of a trance generating loop and the first occurrence of any disabled cognitive function.

trance engineering: The explicit design and construction of trance loops and secondary loops to create specific trances for specific effects.

trance epsilon: The elapsed time between the termination of the trance generating loop and the normalization of any disabled cognitive functions.

trance force: The cause of persistent, resistive, and continuous effects resulting from a trance. The measure of a trance force is the wyrd.

trance generating loop (TGL): Any set of repeated cognitive objects that results in a trance.

trance logic: The perceived effects of distinctive altered or disabled cognitive functions of persons who are in a trance.

trance technology: The methods and applications of the trance model.

tranceling: Any unterminated trance, usually in relation to the unexpected or undesirable effects of such unterminated trances.

trigger: A word or distinctive action that results in the reestablishment of a prior trance.

unhinged trance: A tranceling with no obvious means of control; a compulsion.

wyrd (W): 1. A measure of the power of a trance to resist any change in the effects of the trance. 2. A measure of the ability of a trance to change destiny. 3. A measure of the energy effects of the changes of cognitive functions due to a trance.

About the Author

DENNIS R. WIER IS THE EXECUTIVE Director and Founder of the Trance Research Foundation, Inc. and author of the book *Trance: From Magic to Technology*, which was first published in 1995 and has been reprinted twice and published in German. This second book, *The Way of Trance*, is a continuation of the ideas developed in his first book.

He is a retired computer systems analyst and has been meditating for more than forty years.

Dennis lives in California where he researches trance. He conducts Trance Analysis with clients in Europe, Central America, and the United States. He travels to Europe every year to give talks and workshops on the practical applications of the Trance Model.

Dennis may be contacted through the Trance Research Foundation (www.tranceresearch.org).

About The Trance Research Foundation

The Trance Research Foundation is a non-profit, tax-exempt, educational and research membership organization and is active as a non-governmental organization in Roster Consultative Status with the Economic and Social Council of the United Nations.

Our purpose and mission is to promote awareness of trance worldwide through a variety of important international projects. Among our projects are the development of a uniform drug policy, education and prevention of exploitation of refugees, education of youth regarding trance in order to prevent cult membership, drug abuse and at the same time promoting techniques of meditation which increases personal responsibility and power. Our vision includes the support trance research, to publish books and informational material about trance, trance abuse, mind control, conflict resolution and many other subjects. Another important activity is providing trance analysis and training trance analysts, addiction counselors, training meditation and hypnosis teachers. We also publish the Journal of Trance Research.

The Trance Research Foundation actively solicits tax-deductible financial contributions to support our research, publications and other projects. Details of all our current projects can be found by sending an email to info@trance.edu, downloading the appropriate pdf and printing it locally.

Membership is also an important part of the Trance Research Foundation. Members host workshops, organize presentations, and pot-luck discussion and meditation groups worldwide. Members are an active and integral part of the Trance Research Foundation, and some members may provide local trance analysis services in their community and internationally.

For more information on our activities or membership, visit our web site at www.trance.edu or www.tranceresearch.org or send a blank email to info@trance.edu.

CPSIA information can be obtained at www.ICGtesting.com
Printed in the USA
LVOW041451070213

319134LV00004B/82/P